SCILLYBEAT

Memoirs of a Scilly Copper
(1963–1995)

Roger Jacob

Published by
Jacob
Sticklepath Court   Barnstaple

British Library Cataloguing-in-Publication Data.
A catalogue record for this book is available
from the British Library.

The flag on the front of this cover is that of the Council of the Isles of Scilly. The logo on the flag has the Bishop Rock Lighthouse in the centre, with Star Castle, an old listed building on the islands, on the top left and a daffodil in the top right, one of the most synonymous flowers to the islands. The flag is nicknamed 'Old Smiley' because of its similarities to a smiling face when observed from a distance.

ISBN 978-1-5262-0229-1
Printed in Great Britain by
Arthur H. Stockwell Ltd
Torrs Park   Ilfracombe
Devon EX34 8BA

CONTENTS

John Bourdeaux (Scillonian and alchemist),
The Pottery, St Mary's, Isles of Scilly.

PROLOGUE

SETTING THE SCENE

This memoir is that of a young police officer, in the sixties, being posted to an island community that had been 'self-policed' in a most unconventional manner prior to 1947 and where community policing existed in its most natural and organic format and long before it became a buzzword and initiative of choice on the mainland.

It sets out to encapsulate a snapshot of policing through the eyes of a fledgling young police officer, not long out of his probationary period, who was still learning his trade, and about himself come to that, and in an anecdotal and often humorous way describes the manner in which policing seamlessly integrated into the rhythm of a self-contained community – law and order prevailed by true consent and with the expressed will and support of the people. It must also be said that a considerable amount of humour, sarcasm, wit, tact and diplomacy came into play as a means of retaining the peace and maintaining order.

The book evolves to enlarge, develop and elucidate the selfsame officer's close association with the Isles of Scilly right throughout his lengthy police career and thereafter and how his love for the islands has developed and grown as a consequence.

This memoir is very much designed to be light-hearted and capture the less than serious side of life, sometimes to the detriment of the author's reputation (and others with genuinely no offence intended), but from which he personally developed and grew in stature and standing to become the person he is today. Life is a journey during which many lessons are learnt and personalities developed – this is such a journey that is still ongoing.

Following on from this prologue that incidentally I am delighted to have been asked to pen is an introductory 'chapter' about the Isles of Scilly that I am confident readers will enjoy whether they are fully conversant with the islands or not. Roger was well known to me while he was originally stationed on the Isles of Scilly and in fact taught me to drive. We are of a similar age, and have, over the years, grown to share a comparable philosophy of life. Coupled with a mutual regard and respect for others, lawfulness and democracy – with maybe a touch of irreverence and sarcasm thrown in – we always try to view and live our lives in a light-hearted, convivial and carefree manner. Life is to be lived, after all!

Finally, and by way of completeness, at the end of the book can be found a number of appendices that set out a brief 'History of Policing of the Isles of Scilly', a 'History of the Cornwall Constabulary' and a summary of the life of the author.

It is sincerely hoped that you will enjoy this narrative of nostalgia, musings and recollections of 'better days' and of a place that is very special to the author, although you would never know it by reading this book!

John Bourdeaux (Scillonian and alchemist),
The Pottery, St Mary's, Isles of Scilly.

INTRODUCTION

THE ISLES OF SCILLY:
IN A NUTSHELL

The Isles of Scilly, or Fortunate Isles as they are known, form an archipelago off the south-western tip of the Cornish peninsula consisting of five populated islands, St Mary's, Tresco, St Martin's, St Agnes and Bryher, and many small rocky islets (around 140 in total) lying forty-five kilometres (twenty-eight miles) off Land's End. They are all composed of granite of early Permian age. The population of all the islands at the 2011 census was 2,203.

Offshore, midway between Land's End and the Isles of Scilly, is the supposed location of the mythical lost land of Lyonesse, referred to in Arthurian literature.

The position of the islands causes great contrasts. The warming effect of the sea means they rarely have frost or snow. This allows local farmers to grow flowers earlier than they would be grown on mainland Britain. The chief agricultural product is cut flowers, mostly daffodils.

Exposure to Atlantic winds means that spectacular winter gales lash the islands from time to time and this is reflected in the landscape. On Tresco, the lush subtropical Tresco Abbey Gardens shelters on the southern end of the island, but the low heather and bare rock get the wind on the exposed northern end.

The adjective 'Scillonian' is sometimes used for people or things related to the archipelago.

Scilly forms part of the ceremonial county of Cornwall although it is governed by its own unitary authority and has been since 1890. Since the passing of the Isles of Scilly Order 1930, this authority has had the status of a county council and today is known as the Council of the Isles of Scilly.

In 1834 the Duchy of Cornwall leased the Isles of Scilly to a Hertfordshire squire, Augustus Smith, who became the Lord Proprietor of the islands. He helped bring prosperity to Scilly that is still enjoyed today. He built his home, Tresco Abbey, alongside the ruins of an old priory and set about creating a world-class garden containing plants from all over the world. Successive generations have built upon his legacy and Tresco Abbey Gardens is now internationally renowned as one of the finest subtropical flora and fauna collections in the northern hemisphere.

The vast majority of the population, 1,600, live on St Mary's. The figure has remained stable for the last 100 years, but over the past ten years the number of elderly residents has increased by around seven per cent while those under sixteen have decreased by six per cent. Diversity issues are focused on access to services for the small off-island communities and the influx of seasonal migrant workers which number in excess of 100, predominantly from Eastern Europe.

The Duchy of Cornwall owns the vast majority of land on the islands, apart from a small area of the main town on St Mary's. There are just over a 100 council houses and a key issue is providing sufficient affordable and key-worker housing.

Transportation links involve a ferry service from Penzance which is limited to freight in the winter. Fixed-wing air links are restricted during the winter, but in the summer services are provided through small light aircraft flying from three regional airports, namely Land's End, Newquay and Exeter. Transport between the islands is via small, privately run boats.

The cost of living is high with property and transport prices significantly exceeding the average across the rest of the UK. Incomes are lower than the national or regional average, but there is no unemployment, with many residents undertaking multiple occupations. Education levels are considerably higher than the national average; Five Islands School provides primary and secondary education on the islands with post-sixteen further and higher education undertaken on the mainland.

The Council of the Isles of Scilly delivers the widest range of services of any council in the country; all of the usual statutory services as well as some additional services such as tourism (the economy is eighty-five per cent dependent on this), water and sewerage and operates St Mary's Airport, the tenth busiest regional passenger airport in the UK. This wide range of services is delivered with a limited budget and a small core of staff.

Safeguarding the islands' precious environment is an ever present consideration in the council's deliberations. The whole of Scilly has been designated as an Area of Outstanding Natural Beauty, a Conservation Area and Heritage Coast. Scilly contains both a Special Area of Conservation (EU Habitats Directive) and a Special Protection Area (EU Birds Directive). Taken together this means the islands constitute an EU Natura 2000 site.

The islands enjoy a strong sense of community cohesion and there are high levels of safety and freedom from not only crime itself, but also fear of crime. In fact, the findings from a 2001/2002 Crime Audit for the Isles of Scilly established that the fear of crime did not appear to be a major concern among local residents and the business community despite crime rates having risen in recent years. It was said that the Isles of Scilly remain 'the land that crime forgot'. It is clear, however, that the local residents-and-business community has no intention of being complacent as it continues to demonstrate a desire to explore a wide range of crime-prevention and crime-reduction measures.

Scilly has been inhabited since the Neolithic period; people lived off what they could get from the land or the sea. Scilly had its maritime heyday in the nineteenth century. The beaches were sites for shipbuilding and the harbours were packed with fishing and trading boats.

Farming and fishing continue today, but the main industry now is tourism. Because of the mild climate that the Isles of Scilly experiences, the tourist season is quite long and over the last year or so the islands have also become quite a magnet for numerous cruise ships; they moor up off St Mary's in a stretch of deep water known as 'The Road' or at the rear of St Mary's again in deep water off Porth Hellick Point.

Visitors are attracted to the Isles of Scilly not only to experience a unique and enigmatic style of island life and its mild climate, but also to check out its wide variety of wildlife both at sea and on land. Atlantic grey seals can be found almost at will on both the eastern and western isles and on the many uninhabited islands that are dotted throughout the archipelago, as can numerous land and sea birds. Although a wide range of passage migrants use Scilly as a halting place in spring and autumn, Scilly has only about sixty breeding species and about fifteen of these are seabirds.

At sea the harmless basking shark can sometimes be seen around the Isles of Scilly as can porpoises and common dolphins.

It is believed that the Vikings called the islands 'Syllorgar' and that the Romans named them 'Sully', meaning the sun islands. The letter 'c' was added to the name sometime in the sixteenth century. The first settlers arrived from Cornwall more than 4,000 years ago. They constructed settlements, burial chambers and monuments, many of which can still be seen. Remains found on the now uninhabited island of Nornour are from at least three centuries of Roman occupation, from the first to the third centuries AD. Various artefacts, including coins and brooches, are now on display in the museum on St Mary's.

In the Middle Ages and later, fortifications were built to protect Scilly and thus the mainland from potential invaders, including the French and Spanish. Castles were built, the most impressive being the Star Castle on St Mary's.

It is likely that until relatively recent times the isles were much larger with many of them joined into one island, named Ennor. Rising sea levels flooded the central plain around AD 400–500, forming the current islands.

The Isles of Scilly form part of the Devon and Cornwall Police force area. There is a police station in Hugh Town, St Mary's. The Cornwall Air Ambulance helicopter provides cover to the islands; there are also full-time Westcountry Ambulance Service Trust (WAST) paramedics and ambulance personnel stationed on St Mary's and there is a Medical Launch based at St Mary's that is used by the doctors, WAST and nursing staff based at the local hospital/health centre. The islands have their own independent fire brigade, known as the Isles of Scilly Fire and Rescue Service, which is staffed entirely by retained firefighters on all the inhabited islands.

It is hoped that this brief introduction has set the scene sufficiently for the reader to now enjoy what is to follow. It is the memoir of a way of life that began fifty years ago as seen initially through the eyes of a young police officer. Although the Isles of Scilly have moved on and developed since then, it is pleasing to the author especially that it has not done so at the pace of the mainland or, more importantly, to the detriment of this very special and 'fortunate' place.

RNAS Culdrose helicopter airlifting a passenger from cruise ship Braemar *whilst moored in The Road off Samson with* WAST *ambulance launch and passenger launch* Sapphire *in attendance – provided by Joe Pender.*

CHAPTER 1

BECOMING A POLICE OFFICER

I joined the Cornwall Constabulary on 16th September 1963 at the age of eighteen years and 360 days. I was allocated the shoulder number Constable 91. I spent my first week in lodgings in Bodmin and during the working day was fitted out with uniform and various accoutrements and received a number of briefings. I had left my home in Newquay on Monday 16th September to travel to Bodmin and was home again by the Friday – it was my nineteenth birthday on the Saturday.

On the following Sunday, now nineteen years of age, I travelled to the Police Training Centre, Chantmarle, Dorset. At that time, the training centre for the South West was a grade-1 listed manor house, known as Chantmarle Manor; it was totally isolated within its own grounds, had a moat and was near a village called Cattistock. I got to know all the lanes in and around Chantmarle quite intimately as we traversed them most mornings on a cross-country run before breakfast supervised by an inspector who was invariably in uniform and driving his car! The alternative to a cross-country run was a physical exercise workout in the courtyard by the clock tower, which was equally as foreboding as the running.

After my three-month initial training I returned to Cornwall and originally my father's home in Newquay – I was now looking forward to putting all that I had learnt into practice. I soon discovered, however, that policing in reality was far distant from acting out scenarios and being taught legislation and procedures in a classroom environment.

My first official engagement was to meet the Assistant Chief Constable, Ken Julian, at force headquarters, Bodmin, and in order to do so I travelled up to Bodmin from Newquay. I was intending to travel to Falmouth thereafter, where I had already received an official posting. However, once the ACC realised that a colleague who was being posted to Penzance had just left the Humphrey Davy Grammar School there, he moved him to Falmouth and me to Penzance.

I was using my father's car to make these journeys and I was beginning to wonder how I would break the news to him especially as I was using his petrol. I had also run his car off the road as I neared Goss Moor on the way to Bodmin from Newquay due to a touch of ice on the road, but fortunately I just slid onto a grass verge. After putting a couple of the car's rubber mats under the rear wheels I managed to extricate the car from off the slippery grass and mud and get back on my journey gladly, with no damage to the car or major delay in my journey – it was just my pride that was dented.

After my appointment with the Assistant Chief Constable, I left force headquarters at Bodmin, having reprogrammed in my head the necessary route – there were no such gadgets as satnavs in those days – and I eventually arrived at Penzance Police Station where I met Chief Inspector Alfie Jenkins. I believe it was the first time I had ever been to Penzance! During his introductory speech of welcome he realised that I had not been officially sworn in as a constable – you had to be nineteen years of age to be a sworn constable – and sent me home for the Christmas holidays. There had been no opportunity for me to be sworn in at training school. You can imagine my father's face when I arrived back home in Newquay again on the same day I had left to embark on a new chapter of my life.

All good things, however, come to an end and on returning to Penzance after Christmas I was swiftly sworn in by a magistrate and immediately got to work. I enjoyed an eventful and rewarding time in Penzance and, as the only probationary constable for a while, got involved in many an interesting case and worked closely with CID and traffic officers. I well remember one case that a colleague of mine, Harold Thompson, and I detected during a night shift. We visited Penzance harbour near the railway station, following a tip-off, and noted that a camper van, parked adjacent to the quay wall, had an electric cable coming away from the rear of the vehicle and up to a street light where it was plugged in! Inside the van we could hear the sound of a TV. On knocking on the window the door was opened and it became abundantly clear that the TV was being powered by electricity being illegally taken from the street light! An arrest ensued and the necessary paperwork followed.

My lodgings at Heamoor, near Penzance, were second to none; I lived with the village blacksmith and his wife, Bill and Elizabeth Eddy, and I was treated like a son. My sister Pauline was nursing in London and Bill and Elizabeth's daughter, Caroline, was in her intake – hence me finding these superb lodgings.

Penzance originally had its own Borough Police Force and I had the privilege of working with two former members of that force – Edwin Tapping, who was stationed at Mousehole, and the legendary Johnny Green, who in effect became my tutor constable (he lived near me in Heamoor). Johnny was a larger-than-life character, literally, who was totally respected by all walks of life, especially many of our regular 'customers' who took his word as gospel and never ever crossed him. It was abundantly clear they all had the utmost respect for Johnny as a man, maybe more so than for the uniform he wore.

Johnny always wore his helmet high up on his forehead and what with this and his portly shape it made him resemble what I can only describe as a Toby-jug policeman akin to those that feature on the legendary *Nine Pints of the Law* picture. He certainly taught me a great deal about how to be a good police officer and many of the tricks of the trade, some of which I won't go into now for fear of incriminating myself for the odd 'police regulations' misdemeanour. What I can say though is that 'tea stops' were soon learnt, such as the local bakery and the Queens Hotel on night shift and sometimes a game of snooker in the police station social club was enjoyed once all the properties in Market Jew Street and elsewhere had been checked front and rear. Johnny always used to say, "You need to know what you should be doing if you are ever asked."

Penzance Borough Police had merged with the Cornwall Constabulary in 1947, and in doing so inherited the former force's police boxes or Dr Who Tardises as they would be known today. There were, I believe, three of them: one situated at the railway station, one in Morrab Road to the rear of the Queens Hotel, and another at the entrance to the Treneere Estate near the Humphrey Davy Grammar School. They were great for getting inside out of the cold, wind and rain and for accessing the police station by a direct telephone line. You could also access this telephone from the outside by way of a small hinged door – the public could also use them in this manner – and I well recall having my arm suddenly grabbed by a colleague, who was, unknown to me, inside the box at the railway station one dark and miserable night. It gave me quite a fright but was part of the probationary constable initiation ritual.

While at Penzance you were often placed on guardroom duties that involved meeting and greeting the public, dealing with lost/found property, checking driving documents, answering the telephone and both redirecting incoming and facilitating outgoing calls – you also had to keep the boiler stoked up with coal on night shift. The telephone system was very antiquated, even for those days, and involved the pulling out of wires and plugs and placing them in the necessary extension number and then turning a handle that rang a bell. It also acted in reverse in that telephone extensions throughout the building had to lift their receiver and then request the operator to provide them with an outgoing line. Just to add some spice to the workload of an unsuspecting probationary constable it would be quite a common practice for mischievous and playful officers to lift up several extension telephones at once so that their allotted flap would drop and ring at the switchboard. Answering so many calls at once often put the operator in a bit of a spin.

There was a very similar system at the Police Training Centre, Chantmarle, and one weekend I had the dubious pleasure of manning the office and with this onerous responsibility came the operation of the telephone system! Those officers who had to stay at weekends – you normally only had from lunchtime Saturdays to midnight Sundays off – were allocated administrative and office duties just so as to while away your leisure (and study) time. It also ensured you didn't ponder too much over the fact you couldn't get home for some well-earned time off like most of your colleagues who lived considerably closer. I distinctly recall spending all weekend, when in the office, dreading that the telephone might ring and then having to deal with an internal call from the centre's commandant when my hands were fully engaged in polishing my highly polished boots and my hands were covered in black boot polish – I got away with it but it did add some pressure to the occasion.

Back to Penzance! I did turn the tables on one of my mischievous colleagues one very quiet Sunday evening when I was encouraged – by a more senior constable, I hasten to add – to telephone two outside numbers at once, one being Constable Edwin Tapping at Mousehole Police Station and the other a pub at Madron, the next village on from Heamoor. You can well imagine the conversation that ensued. Each answered almost simultaneously and inquired the purpose of the call from the other. A conversation something like: "Well, you rang me" and "No, I didn't – you rang me" took place. We were listening in at the switchboard and finding it very difficult to stifle a laugh. I eventually pulled out both plugs and cut the calls off – shouldn't have done it, I suppose, but idle hands make light work.

From all this type of shenanigan and tomfoolery I soon learnt that you had to be able to take a joke, have a sharp sense of humour and be able to handle yourself if you were going to survive as a police officer. There was no recognition or acceptance in those days of such things as post-incident stress disorder – or just stress, come to that. It was seen as a weakness – and this type of day-by-day banter, humour, often sarcasm and unique camaraderie ensured you 'lived to fight another day'. These newly acquired skills certainly equipped me more than anything else for what was to come on the Isles of Scilly.

I also learnt very quickly at Penzance that life didn't exist in a simple clear-cut format and that criminals came in all shapes and sizes. In my short time there a local doctor was arrested by the CID on suspicion of performing unlawful abortions and a police colleague, based elsewhere in West Cornwall, was arrested for stealing money from a garage where he had been moonlighting with a second job. Working as a young police officer in Penzance was one of the steepest learning curves of my career, but it quickly taught me never to accept things at face value, never to be judgemental, always to have an open and deeply inquiring mind and most of all, to be fair and compassionate. Some of these attitudes, I am afraid (for example a deep and inquiring mind), never quite leave you, much to the chagrin of my wife, family and close friends.

During my time in Penzance I saved enough to buy my own car. It cost the princely sum of £45, which represented almost my monthly wage – although for the first month or two my father, Bill, came to pick me up after my shift, sometimes at 2 a.m., and return me to Penzance after my rest days, spent happily in Newquay. My father was a widower; my mother, Muriel, died suddenly and unexpectedly when I was sixteen years of age and in the middle of taking my O levels, and although Dad was of ill-health he worked full-time as a shop assistant in a local chemist shop, specialising in cameras, and was the divisional superintendent of the Newquay St John Ambulance Brigade. My sister, Pauline, and I had also joined the St John Ambulance as cadets and later the adult division and this stood us both in good stead as she became a nurse and for me, as a police officer, first-aid skills came in very handy. I still remain a member of the St John Ambulance with fifty-eight years or so to my name.

While still stationed at Penzance, I attended my final continuation two-week course in Folkestone, and towards the end of my time there I received a notification from my father that he had heard I had been posted to Camborne, although nothing officially came to me from within the force. However, on my return home on a Friday night, after a long and tortuous journey from Kent – there were no motorways as such in those days – I was advised by my father that I needed to telephone Camborne

Police Station urgently, only to be told that I must report for duty at 6 a.m. on the Saturday! These were times when you just did as you were told, but even the supervisory diehards of those days were compassionate enough to reach a compromise and I was given a twenty-four-hour stay of execution – I was to report for duty at 6 a.m. on the Sunday.

As you can probably guess, all of this came as a great shock to me, and also to my adopted 'parents' at Heamoor. I had to visit them on the Saturday, pack up my belongings at both my digs and the police station and move up to Camborne and settle into new lodgings.

On a positive note, I was soon confirmed in my appointment as a substantive – 'proper' in Cornish lingo – constable and within a week or so was settled into a new working regime. My posting to Camborne, however, soon brought with it some consolations, one of which was an offer, out of the blue, to move to the Isles of Scilly as the summer seasonal constable for the period April–September 1966.

I knew roughly of the whereabouts of the Isles of Scilly, but beyond that little else. While stationed at Penzance I was aware of the ferry, the *Scillonian*, that sailed daily in the summer from the quay to the Scillies and returned each evening and of the heliport at Eastern Green, from where helicopters flew to St Mary's most days. I believe the heliport was quite a recent innovation and helicopter flights, unlike the *Scillonian* to a degree, were very much affected by bad weather, especially fog.

We had a sergeant at Penzance known as Frank 'Herbie' Short and he was renowned for getting his words mixed up. On arriving at work one day he said to me, "Had a bit of a to-do at the heliport today, boy – a helicopter in flight developed a fault and in order to land safely had to go over Mounts Bay and jeopardise some of his fuel." He meant, of course, jettison! He was also a keen photographer and went to Land's End one day to photograph a recently wrecked boat. On returning to the police station he said, "Got an 'an'some picture of that wreck. It was siliconed against a beautiful blue sky!" The word silhouetted was in his head, but siliconed came out! He was, however, a great character, well respected by both colleagues and the public alike and a good first-aid competition competitor. I can distinctly recollect, while a young constable and competing with him as a member of the Cornwall Police First Aid Team, hearing him say to a competition judge, "I have examined the casualty and I am going to treat the most sincerest injury first!" I am sure the judge knew what Herbie meant as it is a rule of thumb in first-aid to thoroughly examine any casualty and then treat the most serious injury first. Mind you, as age catches up with us all many a 'Herbieism' comes out!

My posting to the Isles of Scilly, needless to say, was a posting that I could not turn down and I found myself on 1st April 1966, All Fools' Day, arriving at St Mary's harbour on board the MV *Scillonian*. I had all my worldly goods in the hold of the ship and undoubtedly a puzzled and worried expression on my face together with a sense of wonderment and awe at what I was letting myself in for! I needn't have worried – it was a posting that was to make a man of me and took me to a place that has remained a treasured memory and a place that I now cherish and call my second home.

Rough seas during winter gales near Mermaid Inn, St Mary's –
provided by Joe Pender and taken by Dave Sherris.

CHAPTER 2

ARRIVING ON THE ISLES OF SCILLY

Policing on the Scillies in those days was described as a country station although the police station itself was also the home of the resident senior constable, Barry Cutler, his wife, Jean, and their poodle dog, Penny. There was also a married constable, Roger Maddern, who lived with his wife, Maureen, in a block of flats, Godolphin Flats, opposite the church in Church Street; this was a relatively new acquisition by the force as the usual complement of the police on the islands was a senior constable who lived in the police station and a single man who lived in lodgings. Barry, if my memory serves me correctly, originally moved to St Mary's as the senior constable, but was promoted to sergeant immediately prior to a royal visit by the Queen and about the time when the Cornwall Constabulary merged with the Devon and Exeter and Plymouth City Police Forces – becoming the Devon and Cornwall Constabulary. Barry was, I believe, the first sergeant on Scilly.

I was to be the summer seasonal constable and by doing so raised the complement of the force by fifty per cent. This was to prove to be a very interesting topic when I had my first encounter with the then prime minister, Harold Wilson, who had a bungalow on St Mary's and visited regularly.

The quay on St Mary's on my arrival was a throng of activity. The harbour itself was full of pleasure craft and launches and the quay was littered with crates, forklift trucks and a mass of dockers grabbing mooring ropes and lifting a walkway up to the side of the *Scillonian*. It suddenly hit me that I had come to work in a place that was very different from what I had been used to and that I would have to learn to handle myself very quickly if I was to survive.

There was no quick fix of a patrol car coming to your aid or a CID officer to support you with a complicated crime investigation. I needn't have worried – every local became my eyes and ears and they were always there at my back for support if required.

My first point of call on St Mary's was my lodgings that I would come to call my home for the next six months. It was a small end-of-terrace cottage on The Strand called 'Puffins' and it was situated right next door to the school and to the rear of the lifeboat house and slipway. It was primarily a small bed-and-breakfast establishment that was run by a lady called Joyce Pim who had two corgi dogs. My room was relatively small yet adequate, especially as I was, over the next six months, always the last person to come in at night – there was an IN/OUT board for each room – either working late or socialising at the Mermaid Inn.

Although I wasn't working that day officially, I did call at the police station that was situated on The Parade, near the Town Hall and opposite the park, to familiarise myself with the facilities available. I was given a key to the front door of Barry and Jean's house and shown the police office that was at the end of the ground-floor corridor close to the back door and Barry and Jean's kitchen. The back door led out into a rear yard where there was one cell. The cell was pretty much used by Barry as a garden shed although during my time we did actually house a few prisoners in it – more of that later. Barry also used the step of the cell on one occasion to facilitate the mating of his petite and beloved poodle Penny with a young, immature but much larger poodle dog that belonged to a neighbour. Once the deed was done the young stud left in rather a hurry, sprinting across the back garden, scaling the wall at the end and returning to his home under his own steam. Sadly, Penny's pregnancy didn't end up as Barry and Jean had wished – the birth of the resulting puppies was traumatic and although they all sadly died, Penny did survive but only after a scare or two.

I am told that this particular house was acquired as the official police station in the early 1940s, but that it then had no cell. This was housed in the Town Hall and this was sometimes occupied when dances and other functions were being held there. This must have led to many interesting situations occurring when functions were being held, especially when you consider the type of offences for which the prisoner was incarcerated! All this changed, however, in 1953 when a single cell was erected at the back of the police station on The Parade at a cost of £525. It is said in a local record held at the Isles of Scilly Museum that 'inmates of this particular cell have been few due to the tact and resourcefulness with which island constables have maintained law and order.' A compliment indeed!

Later that night I accompanied Roger Maddern on patrol with the prime function being, as I thought, to ensure the public houses closed on time. Roger was in uniform and I was in civilian clothing. On entering the Mermaid Inn it appeared to me that there were a lot of staff milling around with customers and generally tidying up – emptying ashtrays, etc. – and this seemed odd at the time. However, all was soon to be revealed. Once a large number of punters had left, the front door was closed and locked and I was asked what I was having! It transpired that all those people that I mistook for staff were in fact locals and that we were about to be engaged in a sort of lock-in! Having said that, no money changed hands and the drinks were dispensed to the locals on a reciprocal basis for services rendered. I soon learnt that not everything costs money on Scilly and that locals operated on a 'You help me and I will help you' basis. What a baptism of fire for my first day on Scilly!

St Mary's harbour from Porthloo showing lifeboat house and slipway.

CHAPTER 3

SETTLING IN ON THE ISLANDS

My first day in uniform and being on patrol was quite an experience. Everybody I passed offered me their 'hand of friendship' – especially the locals, whom I immediately took to my heart. Each and every one of them had a great and unique sense of humour and always carried a beaming smile on their face. I soon made many friends and acquaintances and quickly got to know the lie of the land.

Visits to St Mary's quay, to basically ensure that pleasure boats weren't overloaded (we had copies of each boat's Board of Trade licence) were a regular occurrence, but by and large the members of the St Mary's Boatmen's Association were law abiding and fully conscious of their responsibilities – at least they were when we were present! I was, however, to encounter a situation where we had to take action for a boat being overloaded, but I will come to that later.

I soon learnt that we had no official means of police transport on the islands apart from foot patrol. Having said that, most of the places we needed to get to were within Hugh Town, the main centre of population on St Mary's, and if not we could always commandeer my landlady's car. Barry Cutler had taught Joyce Pim to drive and in recompense she had made her old Austin, or maybe it was a Morris Minor, available, with a key being kept at the police station for use in an emergency. I believe that Barry was included on Joyce's car insurance, but as a young officer with a less than inquiring mind at that time I didn't think of checking – I would have now!

On my first Sunday, Roger Maddern decided that he ought to show me around St Mary's after lunch and from somewhere produced two pedal cycles – I have no idea where he got them from to this day. St Mary's only has about nine miles of road, so we couldn't get lost! We set off, I believe in a clockwise direction, and eventually ended up at the airport near Old Town, which on Sundays was normally closed.

There was no way of arriving or leaving the islands on a Sunday, by boat or air, but on this occasion the airport office was open and there was a plane on the Tarmac. We got into conversation with the pilot of the plane, a small two-winged, propeller-type plane, and he said he could take us up for a ride if we liked. We hurriedly agreed and with an air of excitement got into the seats immediately behind the cockpit. The pilot jumped in as well, fired up the engines and off we took, at great speed into the blue and cloud-free sky. Once we were airborne we got into conversation with the pilot only to ascertain that this was his first visit to the islands and that his reason for coming was to practise some 'circuits and bumps' so as to familiarise himself with the landing strip. He was apparently contemplating the delivery of papers on a Sunday as a little business venture and we had become part of his rehearsal! The landing strips on St Mary's Airport are apparently difficult to negotiate because of the upward and downward draughts of the wind off the sea and against the contours of the cliffs and our pleasure flight had turned into a bit of a potential disaster. In this day and age we perhaps might have done a risk assessment!

The flight did however illustrate to me how beautiful and unique the Isles of Scilly were from the air. I saw for myself the crystal-clear clarity of the water, and the golden sandy beaches that surrounded all the islands. Looking back and very much in hindsight, this short-circuit and bumpy flight that I had undertaken over the entire archipelago had enabled me to view my complete patch in a matter of minutes and in almost one snapshot in time. If I held any doubts or misgivings as to the job ahead, they were immediately dispelled and I began to look forward with much keenness and enthusiasm to what was to follow.

St Mary's Police Station as in 1966.

Pulpit Rock, Peninnis Head, St Mary's.

CHAPTER 4

POLICE TRANSPORT

As I have already said, for police transport, Shanks's pony was the order of the day and if necessary Barry Cutler was able to make use of Joyce Pim's car. Pedal cycles were also to hand, but to be honest I can't recall using one after our trip to the airport and taking our potentially perilous flight. Getting to the other inhabited islands, Tresco, St Martins, Bryher and St Agnes, was by pleasure boat or, in an emergency, a hired vessel, and only then with the permission of the superintendent from Camborne. This only happened to me once, but I will leave this to a later chapter.

There were very few specific reasons during my period on Scilly when we needed to go to an 'off' island, so it became a bit of a lottery as to which one we might visit and patrol. Often it was left to which passenger boat you particularly liked, which way the wind was blowing, how rough the sea was, when the boats were going to return to St Mary's or which boatman might be going to do a bit of fishing on the return journey to St Mary's.

One of the joys of patrolling an 'off' island was to see the bemused faces of some visitors when they saw a uniformed police officer approaching them. They were always intrigued about what sort of problems we encountered and how we managed without backup from elsewhere. To be honest, we did rather tease some of the more gullible visitors and lay it on a bit, but when they found out we were pulling their leg they took it in good humour.

Some visitors were more gullible than others and the boatmen were far more adept at winding them up than us – we learnt from them, of course.

One of the more exciting round-island trips was an excursion to the Bishop Rock Lighthouse then back to St Agnes to land – the lighthouse is approximately seven miles from St Mary's. The Bishop Rock Lighthouse in those days was manned twenty-four hours a day by lighthouse keepers who, from memory, spent two months on then one month off. They and their families were accommodated on St Mary's. The passenger boats used to convey the keepers' mail and often some general provisions and to get them safely across a chasm of 'boiling' rough water a breeches buoy was used. This is also how they used to land and remove the keepers from their period of watch, and I was offered more than once to have a go and land on the lighthouse. I refused, naturally, as I was certain that at some stage the rope on the breeches buoy would be slackened purposely with the end result of me ending up in the ocean in front of eighty or so happy (maybe some green!) holidaymakers all snapping away with their cameras.

Anyway, one of the main concerns of some holidaymakers was how the keepers managed in the winter when the sea was extraordinarily rough. The stock reply from the boatmen was that the lighthouse was towed into St Mary's harbour for the winter where it was much more sheltered – it's amazing how many believed this. Others inquired whether the lighthouse 'went all the way to the bottom of the sea' in the genuine belief that it was a floating object.

The Bishop Rock Lighthouse is now fully automated and has a landing pad on the top for engineers to come and go in a helicopter; I wouldn't have minded getting onto the lighthouse by this means!

One of the best stories I heard, however, and this was relayed to me on many an occasion by the boatman Richard Lethbridge, was a genuine and sincere inquiry from a visitor that went much like this:

"Do these islands grow?"

Richard replied: "In what sense do you mean? We grow daffodils, for example."

The person concerned then, by way of illustration, pointed to a tide mark on the rocks and said, "Well, this morning this mark was much higher up on the rocks."

Richard, in stifling a laugh, said, "I assume you do not live near the coast and have not, therefore, heard of low and high tides."

It is possible that the significance of Richard's statement did not register at the time, but I am sure, when the penny dropped, that the person concerned felt a little stupid! It was a common phrase during the sixties to refer to the many visitors who holidayed on the Cornish coast for the first time as members of the Birmingham Navy, no offence meant. I guess this statement could have applied to this gullible person, who, like most of us, probably felt very stupid at the time but dined out on the story as they matured and could laugh at themselves.

The other forms of transport available to us were of course to and from the mainland by means of the *Scillonian* and her sister ship, the *Queen of the Isles*, and helicopters, all from Penzance. In those days the helicopter only landed on St Mary's, although in later years, before the service stopped altogether, it also landed on Tresco.

As police officers we would always meet the *Scillonian* or *Queen of the Isles* on arrival at the quay and check the passengers on and off. If an undesirable was encountered arriving then he or she was suitably advised not to settle on the islands but to return to the mainland at the first opportunity. I guess this was most probably not legal in those days, although when one undesirable decided to take legal advice from the local solicitor he did remain on St Mary's overnight but left the following day. I guess he was just trying to prove a point.

Having said all this, if the local boatmen or dock workers got wind of what we had said to these individuals then the gentle 'request' of ours was often backed up by them in a much more Anglo-Saxon way than we ever could. I must add, this didn't happen that often – it's a good job that the Human Rights Act didn't exist in those days.

The only official time we used the *Scillonian* or *Queen of the Isles* for police work was when we arrested two young lads for committing a minor crime and after a short period in our cell we bailed them to a forthcoming court on St Mary's. I seem to recollect that we then placed them on the *Scillonian*, from which they were collected by colleagues at the other end on arrival. They were also wanted by the police in Penzance for similar minor crimes and, if my memory serves me correctly, they were eventually dealt with by the Penzance magistrates for both sets of offences. There was no point in escorting them – they only had the Celtic Sea to jump into. We also did this with another male arrested on St Mary's for a criminal act on the mainland and this proved equally successful. Maybe in this day and age a risk assessment might have affected our decision, but it worked out anyway.

In 1966, community policing was very much in its heyday and policing by consent and in partnership with the community was the guiding principle. In the Isles of Scilly this came naturally. It was important for police officers to be highly visible on the streets, and although panda cars became the norm on the mainland it was only to get to those places where foot patrols were impractical or in an emergency. There were police officers stationed at country stations, some with motorcycles, and others with just bicycles, who by and large covered their patch twenty-four hours a day and were often called out in an emergency regardless of what hours they might have already worked that day.

When I was at Penzance, the only mobile resource we had was a couple of trained police motorcyclists who worked opposite shifts to each other and the duty sergeant's personal car. We also had a traffic car based at Penzance, but this was more often than not a county resource and if on nights, for example, had to cover all of Cornwall from Saltash/Torpoint to Penzance and all towns and villages in between. The Penzance traffic car was crewed by Alfie Pittam and Ron Fisher and they would often take me out with them after I had concluded my shift for some extra action. Ron eventually retired in Truro and went on to be the Bishop of Truro's driver for many years.

A keeper being transferred to the Bishop Rock Lighthouse from a boat. He has to be hauled some forty-five feet up to the set-off. On a rough day a ducking for the man on the rope is often inevitable.

Bryher in vicinity of Hell Bay Hotel and Great Porth.

CHAPTER 5

THE BOATMEN

I became very friendly with many of the boatman; there was Ben and David Badcock, Lloyd, Michael, Alfie, Frazer and Gee Hicks, Bill, Frank and Guthrie Pender, Richard Lethbridge, John Nicholls, Lew Hitchens and Peter Thompson, to name but a few. Most of them were members of the St Mary's Boatmen's Association. The association boats that I recall being in use during my time were the *Lily of Laguna*, *Sea King*, *Guiding Star*, *Swordfish*, *Golden Spray*, *Britannia* and *Buccaneer*. John Nicholls and Peter Thompson were, I believe, independent. If I recall it correctly, John's boat was called the *Silver Cloud*. I still know both John and Peter very well; Peter owns and runs, among many things, a fish-and-chip shop near the Town Hall – he used to run The Galley Fish Restaurant above – and John has recently retired as the secretary to the St Mary's Lifeboat and is basically retired. John was a seafarer in his time and did on occasions act as the skipper of the *Scillonian*. Each time I visit I am usually greeted by John shouting out, in my direction, some derogatory and disparaging remark that I return in equal measure!

The St Mary's Boatmen's Association has been in being now for about fifty years; as far as I can recall, it was formed just before the time of my arrival. Basically all the larger boats working from St Mary's come under the umbrella of the association. Today there are about ten boats working within the association and I would guess there was a similar number in my time, with each carrying between seventy-five and 100 passengers. This represents a combined seating capacity of over 800. Each boat is owned and operated by its own skipper; the association enables the boatmen to work together to provide visitors with the best possible service. The association caters for all boating requirements, including direct trips to all of the islands, inhabited or not, as well as wildlife trips to see Atlantic grey seals and breeding seabirds, including puffins. Each inhabited 'off' island has its own boat service, much like St Mary's.

Being a single man I spent a lot of my free time boating, fishing and socialising with the boatmen in the local pubs in the evenings. Many have become lifelong friends – especially Guthrie, who took me under his wing and taught me a lot about good old-fashioned sarcasm, humour and living off your wit; he had a larger-than-life personality and reputation and was an absolute legend in his own lifetime. Guthrie, although no longer with us, is still very much an icon on St Mary's and both listening to and repeating stories about him never bores me and always makes me laugh.

On his gravestone at Old Town Church cemetery he is described as 'Scilly's Last Swashbuckler' and his plot in the graveyard is surrounded by characters such as Lloyd Hicks, Harold Wilson and Ray Gunter, MP, who also loved the islands. Ironically it is rumoured locally on Scilly that Lloyd Hicks was not a supporter of Harold Wilson and I guess he never envisaged being laid to rest so close to him.

I first met Guthrie on St Mary's quay, and although he was at first difficult to understand – he talked very quickly and with a distinct Scillonian lilt – I soon built up an understanding of his pronounced and enigmatic accent and learnt a lot from his down-to-earth and gritty sense of humour and unique lifestyle.

When I first knew him he lived in a fairly substantial garden shed in the rear garden of the Kavorna Café, in Hugh Town, owned by his brother Gilbert, with his dog and worldly goods – including his shotguns – and spent most of his evenings in the Mermaid Inn. Apparently the Kavorna Café was formerly the dairy and this doubled as the family home of the Pender family. Guthrie always sat in the same place in the Mermaid Inn, at a stool against the bar just inside the door, where he amused the visitors – especially a lot of young and beautiful women, who all plied him with beer and the odd tot of rum!

Guthrie now very much lives on in his son, Joe Pender, and his daughter, Catherine. During my time on Scilly Guthrie formed a relationship with, and later married, a hospital nurse called Heather, and Joe and Catherine were their offspring. My colleague Barry Cutler was Guthrie's best man at his wedding – more of Guthrie later.

Bishop Rock Lighthouse.

Porthcressa Beach, St Mary's, looking towards Buzza Tower and Peninnis Head.

'Scilly's Last Swashbuckler', Guthrie Pender – provided by Joe Pender.

CHAPTER 6

SHIFTS

In 1966, police officers who were stationed in country stations worked, more often than not, split shifts – such as 9 a.m. to 1 p.m. and 9 p.m. to 1 a.m.; 7 a.m. to 11 a.m. and 7 p.m. to 11 p.m.; or 8 a.m. to noon and 8 p.m. to midnight – with the odd 9 a.m. to 5 p.m. thrown in, and so on and so forth. It had been agreed by the powers that be at Camborne, however, that although we could plan for such shifts we could vary them as necessary and to suit the needs of policing the islands. There were very rarely more than two officers on duty at once during any working day, so often both would cover the morning shift and then share out the remainder of the day as necessary. Being a single man I was just happy to be out and about and working and on many days worked morning, noon and night, taking the odd hour or two off as necessary. Policing became a way of life and it was fun anyway – why did I want time off? Being a police officer in those days, like many public-service roles, was seen as a vocation or calling and not just a job.

To be absolutely honest there were never any major policing problems to exercise your mind. Traffic was not an issue in those days as so very few locals possessed motor vehicles – totally different nowadays! In fact I only ever recall getting one call at the police station regarding traffic congestion and that, as it turned out, was a spoof call. We were watching the football World Cup Final held at Wembley Stadium at the police station when England beat Germany after extra time and the local butcher, as a wind-up, decided to report a vehicle causing an obstruction outside his shop. His shop was situated in the widest part of the main street through Hugh Town, and so we told him where to go, which in policing jargon was a bit like "Do you like sex and travel?" A bit Anglo Saxon and vague, I agree, but I trust you get my drift! The current butcher's shop is now situated around the corner in Garrison Lane with the former butcher's premises being a very successful bistro and café.

The evening shifts were always pleasurable and the pubs a bed of fun and banter. I got to know the licensee of the Mermaid Inn, Les Smith, quite well and he entrusted me with the keys of his car, a Triumph Herald that he garaged each night near to where I lodged. He kept it outside the pub during the daytime; often I would fetch it for him in the morning and/or garage it at night. Les and the locals introduced me to the drink 'rum and shrub' and it soon became my tipple of choice. To be honest I didn't drink a lot of alcohol before going to the Scillies, but on departure I received my graduation certificate (a 2:1).

At the weekends, discos were held in the Town Hall – records were placed on and off a record deck behind the stage curtain often by whomever was passing and at their discretion. These discos were arranged by different local groups and societies and, despite there being no regular live group or band, were very well attended. The job of a disc jockey became a particular favourite of my colleague Roger Maddern. Roger was a very affable and laid-back character who would invariably leave the police station without his helmet and if he got to the Town Hall and became hooked on record selection then that was that – there was no going back for his helmet; why would you need a helmet if you were a disc jockey? I would just leave him there, go on into town and see out the pubs, and then rejoin him – or, at least, his disc-jockey alter ego.

I never actually attended these discos socially; I didn't consider myself much of a dancer although I was a dab hand at the Cornish 'Floral Dance', having paraded my rhythmic skills on many an occasion through the streets of Newquay as a teenager in top hat and tails as part of a fundraising initiative for Newquay St John Ambulance. My dancing ability is often described now as 'dad dancing'!

All this disco stuff, however, did take me back to my church youth-club days in Newquay when, with some of my schoolmates, we formed a group very much based on The Shadows of Cliff Richard fame; I played rhythm guitar. We had a very good teacher in a guy called John Gould, who later went on to play the piano professionally on TV shows such as *That's Life* and *Play School*. The rest of us never quite attained such fame (infamy maybe), although we did once play at the Newquay St John Ambulance Christmas Dinner/Dance at the Hotel Bristol. There was no *X Factor* or *Britain's Got Talent* in those days, although the phrase 'Don't give up your day job' might have been more relevant.

Back to the Scillies! I thoroughly enjoyed working with Barry and Roger and learnt a lot from them. They were well-rounded and seasoned officers in their own right and I was able to follow their good example of how to competently police within an isolated community yet be firm and positive where necessary. I am pleased to say, however, that although relatively inexperienced I was able to contribute to the team in that I had dabbled with quite a lot of crime investigation in my short career and was au fait with the relevant procedures and paperwork. This came in handy later during my posting.

Fishing boat on beach near the quay, New Grimsby, Tresco.

CHAPTER 7

HAROLD WILSON, PM

I hadn't been on St Mary's very long – it was over the Easter holidays, I believe – when we were advised that Harold Wilson, the then prime minister was to arrive on holiday and stay in his bungalow. I was detailed with Roger Maddern to meet the *Scillonian* and then remain on guard outside the vessel's lounge, where the local civic dignitaries were to meet Harold Wilson and his entourage over a tipple or two. We hadn't been in position very long when the door of the lounge that we were guarding opened and we were invited in, full of trepidation as to the reason why. Harold Wilson had apparently asked to be introduced to us – he was a genial character who immediately relaxed us and we were made to feel at home. He spoke to me first and said, "Do you know that wherever I go in the world I never get 100 per cent turnout of the police force apart from here and now you have arrived it is only two-thirds!' What could I say other than to reassure him that he would receive 100 per cent from all three of us irrespective of only greeting him with two-thirds!'

He visited several times for a holiday during my period on the islands and on each occasion our encounters were memorable. On one occasion I had visited the Mermaid Inn at closing time and, being hungry, bought myself a pasty. I placed it in my right hand and decided to walk to the quay and eat it in privacy. As I turned the corner of the pub to enter the quay I was met by Harold Wilson and his bodyguard coming towards me. I had to swiftly move the pasty to my left hand to allow me to salute the PM, whereupon he said something like "Goodnight, officer – enjoy your pasty!"

On another occasion I was in the paper shop, Mumford's in Hugh Town, behind the counter, engaged in some light banter with Bill Pender's wife, Nora, who worked there, when the PM came in and said, "I hope you are behaving yourself, officer!" I was, of course, but it was somewhat embarrassing to have been caught out acting in a frivolous and jocular manner by the PM.

My most memorable encounter with the PM was probably when he was invited to a beach barbecue on Pelistry Beach, at the rear of St Mary's, by hotel staff and in order to get him there we had to borrow Joyce's car. The last part of the journey was on foot down a dark, stony lane and it was obvious we were going in the right direction when we saw a large bonfire alight on the beach in front of us. Harold Wilson mingled with the partygoers and we kept a close eye on him together with his protection officer – Gordon Fryer, I believe he was called. The partygoers were very relaxed in the PM's company, as was he, and many requested his autograph. Not being the sort of folk to go walking around on a deserted beach in the dead of night with a pen and paper, it fell upon us to provide a small pad of what we termed HO/RT/1 slips that we issued to request a driver to produce his/her driving documents at a police station if they didn't have them with them at the time of request. I do believe that the PM also signed my pocketbook – well, it made a change from the sergeant or inspector signing it when they met you on a point.

Yes, in those days we had to make hourly points at a telephone kiosk or similar location where there was ready access to a telephone, although this did not apply on the Isles of Scilly. You were never far from the police station and each knew where the others were going. Neither did we have the luxury of police radios or mobile phones in those days, just ingenuity, resourcefulness and talking to the public – will this ever catch on again!

Talking of making points at telephone kiosks, one of my favourite locations in Penzance was at the top of Causewayhead, where at about 11 p.m. each night the chip-shop proprietor, at closing time, would hand out to any police officer making a point there a portion of fish and chips. We used to wear capes in those days, so it was quite simple to conceal the food although not the smell! However, one particular night the sergeant arrived just as I had concealed my fish-and-chip supper under my cape and then proceeded to engage me in conversation for ten or fifteen minutes. As he left he said, "Have a good shift and enjoy your fish and chips!' They were, of course, stone cold by now and had to be suitably disposed of.

I also well remember this chip shop for an incident that occurred in the immediate vicinity one Sunday evening when I had driven back to Penzance from a short break in Newquay and where a colleague and I spotted a stolen car in possession of two youths. Chasing the car in my private motor was not an option, but having called the incident in we did support other officers to eventually track down the stolen car at Canonstown, near St Erth, although it did take most of the night to do so. I learnt several years later that one of the youths arrested subsequently murdered a warder at a detention centre where he had been detained for other offences. Maybe we had had a lucky escape?

At Camborne one of the sergeants regularly directed officers to keep a point at telephone kiosks many miles away from the town centre, sometimes at adjoining villages and outside the built-up area. It became a bit of a route march to get from one point to the other in time. I think he had a bit of a mean streak or power outage – you would need a high-vis jacket to do that now and a risk assessment to boot.

Let me digress yet again while the use of HO/RT/1 is still in my mind: I well remember one of the first times I had to use one and it turned out to be quite embarrassing. I was on duty in Camborne High Street, prior to being posted to the Isles of Scilly, when I had cause to stop a mini motor car that was being driven by a young male who was visiting the area on holiday. On requesting his name he said, "Gerald Julius Benjamin Caesar!' I thought at first that he was pulling my leg – many a man spoken to during the Christmas period would give the name 'Father Christmas!' However, on checking his driving licence it was clear that this was his actual name, although he couldn't produce a valid certificate of insurance. I duly gave him a completed HO/RT/1 slip and waved him on his way only to find I had left my pocketbook in the driver's door pocket of his car. Fortunately I was able to track down Julius Caesar quite quickly and my pocketbook was back where it belonged well before I had cause to confess my indiscretion to my sergeant. Needless to say, Julius Caesar did not get reported for any minor motoring offences and I had learnt another lesson.

Right, back to the beach barbecue and the PM! As the merriment continued in a most relaxed and convivial manner, our attention was drawn to a number of screams coming from the direction of the water's edge, where we knew a number of partygoers were swimming – in varying stages of undress, I hasten to add. Harold asked us to shine our torches in the direction of the commotion, whereupon we saw a local farmer, who perhaps ought to remain nameless, sliding out of the water with his back to us and wearing nothing more than his birthday suit – he was well tanned apart from his cheeks, which were lily white, and I am not referring to his face! All I will say about the identity of the brazen and shameless swimmer is that he was quite obviously an admirer of the PM and his family, not necessarily in a political sense, having named twin lambs born on the date of the general election in May 1966 – which Harold Wilson and his Labour Party won handsomely – as Harold and Mary.

We then decided it was time to return the PM to his home and we left only to hear afterwards that one of the partygoers had subsequently endeavoured to pole-vault the fire and had fallen in, badly burning himself although not in a life-threatening way. What would the press have made of that in this day and age?

It is a sign of the times, I suppose, that during the time I spent on the islands Harold Wilson spent each night at his bungalow with his wife Mary, alone, with his single and armed protection officer sleeping in the Old Customs House on The Strand a mile or so away. It was our duty to keep an eye on the bungalow for an hour or so into the early hours of the night and then retire to our beds. In years to follow, when Harold Wilson was a backbencher, and following the Northern Ireland crisis, he attracted a team of full-time Firearms Protection Officers, who kept him under close protection throughout his stays on St Mary's on a twenty-four-hour basis.

I am sure that the peace and tranquillity of the Isles of Scilly, and the fact that Harold Wilson and his family could merge into the background of life on the islands, was a great benefit to a man who held the most senior political position in this country, not once, but twice. Islanders went out of their way to protect that rural idyll that he so richly cherished, to the extent that when John Nott, at a time when he was the prospective Conservative parliamentary candidate for St Ives (which included the Isles of Scilly) visited the islands to canvass support, he unwittingly canvassed the PM's house.

Harold Wilson, his wife, Mary, and family were, without any doubt, steadfast supporters of all things Scilly, with the islands seemingly being rarely out of his mind. While in power, for example, and during question time in the House of Commons in the early seventies and following an exchange about the proposal of the Scottish Nationalist Party that Orkney should be able to become an independent country in its own right, Harold Wilson said, "I only hope that the Isles of Scilly will not declare UDI on the strength of this advocacy."

I was most certainly privileged to have met and known Harold Wilson, if only briefly. He was a PM who, irrespective of the party he represented, was held in high esteem and regarded by most as a personable, affable and charming man. I am not so sure you could say the same about some of our current politicians.

Sir Harold and Lady Wilson have spent many years holidaying in the Isles of Scilly. In fact they brought their family here from an early age. This picture shows them relaxing on Samson with their youngest son, Giles.

Loaded Camel Rock at Porth Hellick, St Mary's – see Chapter 8.

CHAPTER 8

MEMORABLE CRIME INVESTIGATIONS

Crime per se was not a major problem on the Scillies. Incidents involving minor offences of vandalism did, however, and on occasions, make the headlines in the local *Scillonian Magazine*. For example, on one night several cars were tampered with in and around Hugh Town and deckchairs on Porthcressa Beach were taken from the bank and laid out across the beach. Not the crimes of the century, it has to be said, but niggling nevertheless to a community that rarely experienced such behaviour. 'This Is Not the Sort of Thing One Expects in Scilly' was the headline in the magazine.

I do, however, recall getting involved in a number of notable crimes, beginning with the arrest of a man for being drunk and incapable. He had apparently locked himself in the toilets on the quay after a good night out, and when found and released by two crew members of the *Queen of the Isles* had consumed two bottles of whisky. Needless to say, he was legless but very happy. He was fined £1 by the magistrates on the following day and I am not so sure now that the toilet door was locked in the first place.

At the other end of the scale I was involved in a protracted and most unusual and interesting shipwrecking case. Many different types of vessels come into St Mary's harbour throughout the summer – many more now than in my time. In fact, a visit by a German yacht in the summer of 1966 was the subject at the time of a 'Scilly Snap' entry in the *Scillonian Magazine* to mark the unique occasion.

One boat that did visit in my time was the MFV *Sanu*, sixty-two tons, owned by the author Denys Val Baker; he lived in St Ives and was a Welsh writer, specialising in short stories, novels, and autobiographies – he also promoted the arts. The *Sanu* had the appearance of a converted trawler and Denys Val Baker, after having spent some time moored up in St Mary's harbour, moved up to the Tresco Channel on Saturday 4th May and set anchor quite close to Cromwell's Castle. She became a bit of a focal point for the passenger boats and an item of much interest to the visitors.

Yet it appears that when Mr Baker, his wife and some friends/crew returned to the boat, having gone ashore on Tresco for the evening, they found that the boat had dragged her anchor and was half full of water. Crew members recovered their sleeping gear and then spent half the night in Cromwell's Castle. At about 3 a.m. the St Mary's lifeboat arrived on the scene and took the shipwrecked party back to St Mary's, where meals and accommodation were arranged by the local Shipwrecked Mariners' Society.

Early on the Sunday morning we were advised of the incident and we did attend the scene to monitor and assist where necessary. Divers inspected the underneath of the vessel and found they could not repair the badly holed *Sanu* until they had lifted her out of the water. At some stage she was righted on a rising tide and pumped out while the holes were temporarily repaired. This was done, I believe, after the vessel had been pulled onto a stony beach alongside Cromwell's Castle.

It was a glorious morning and the wreck attracted many a happy-snappy holidaymaker. The lifeboat crew did all they could to salvage as much as possible of the valuable property on board, having to leave at some stage because of the loss of daylight. They returned next day to continue with their salvage operation.

To our great surprise we were soon to receive a complaint from the owner that some expensive and valuable equipment, which had not been salvaged by the crew of the lifeboat the previous day, had been stolen from within the vessel overnight. There was, as I remember it, a ship's compass, a hand compass, a pair of binoculars, echo-sounding equipment, rope and a ship's horn missing at a total cost of about £150.

It was now a job for us and we commenced door-to-door inquiries on both Bryher and Tresco. After a fruitless day, apart from detecting that a number of locals had picked up quite a lot of mundane property that had been washed up and away from the vessel since the sinking (in other words flotsam), we were about to call it a day when bingo! As we passed a certain house on Tresco we were 'advised' – more like a 'psst', I suppose – to go and check the coal bunker at the back of a house of a lad we had previously interviewed, and that if we did so we might be in luck. How right that informant was!

It was getting very late in the day and after summoning a lift back to St Mary's in a boat owned by a resident of Bryher we decided to continue with our inquiries the following day. On returning to St Mary's Police Station, with the goods recovered from the coal bunker, I received a telephone call from a resident of Bryher whom we had previously interviewed as a possible suspect. He readily confessed that he had some of the stolen gear and that he would put it on a boat and send it over to us as soon as possible. He was duly advised, in no uncertain terms, that this was not the way we worked, and arrangements were made to return to Bryher the following day to recover the stolen goods and interview him.

We had cracked the case and the paperwork began. After some research of the law books I soon realised that this was no average theft – or larceny, as it was called in those days – but a theft from a stranded vessel or, in layman's terms, shipwrecking. Furthermore it was not an offence that could be dealt with at the local magistrates' court, but had to go for trial at quarter sessions, the nearest one being at Penzance.

This story, as you can imagine, caused quite a bit of interest in the press – headlines like 'Scilly Pirates' or 'Pirates of Scilly' became quite common. Because of the mode of trial it was necessary to arrange a specific court in the Town Hall, presided over by local magistrates supported by a magistrates' clerk from the mainland, to hear the evidence and record it all by way of typed depositions. From memory, it took about three days at least to do this and then it became a waiting game until the case came up for listing at Penzance Quarter Sessions.

Both of the local men who had been charged eventually pleaded guilty to the charge, an offence in contravention of Section 64 of the Larceny Act (replaced soon after by the Theft Act) – each man was fined £50. All the stolen property had been recovered and the offenders' remorse ensured they were leniently dealt with.

The *Sanu* was most certainly not in the league of Scilly's most famous wreck, HMS *Association*, which perished on the Gilstone in 1707. The Fleet Admiral, Sir Cloudesley Shovel, and 2,000 men (some records claim 800) were drowned in this disaster; the *Association* is reputed to have been carrying bullion and many a diver has gone in search of it ever since. I believe some artefacts are now housed at the Isles of Scilly Museum and there is a plaque on the beach at Porth Hellick where Sir Cloudesley Shovel's body is alleged to have washed ashore and where it was initially buried. However, by order of Queen Anne the body was later exhumed and subsequently carried in state to London. During the journey from the West Country large crowds turned out to pay their respects and he was finally interred in Westminster Abbey on 22nd December 1707.

There is, however, a further theory as to how Sir Cloudesley Shovel met his untimely end. Local legend has it that Shovel was alive when he reached the shore of Scilly at Porth Hellick, but was murdered by a woman for the sake of his priceless emerald ring. At that time the Scillies had a wild and lawless reputation. This theory has, however, been discounted by the historians as there is no indication that the ring was recovered and the legend stems from a romantic and unverifiable deathbed confession. Good story nevertheless!

I wasn't aware of this alternative theory until recently when I read a book entitled *Name to a Face* by Robert Goddard. It was the book's cover that initially caught my attention – it had a picture on it of what I immediately recognised as the Camel Rock, which is one of the outstanding features of Porth Hellick

Cove. It was a most interesting read and took me back to my spiritual home, the Scillies.

Although I cannot remember the actual date of the *Sanu* court case, it did take place on a day when one of my colleagues was tragically killed on duty near Camborne while riding his police motorcycle. This tragic event, especially his untimely death, stayed with me throughout my career as it was he who had provided me with a handmade leather case, made by a friend of his, in which I kept my duty pocketbook. I used this throughout my career and until the day I retired.

In researching for this particular story I came across a letter from the owner of the *Sanu*, Denys Val Baker, in an edition of the *Scillonian Magazine*. In summary it thanks the various islanders who kindly helped in the raising of his boat, specifically Matt Lethbridge (cox of the St Mary's lifeboat) and crew, shipwrights and riggers of the Isles of Scilly Steamship Company, divers, officers and men of the St Mary's Fire Brigade, the skippers and crews of the various local boats that had assisted, coastguards on Tresco, the Lloyd's agent and the local representative of the Shipwrecked Mariners' Society. In the letter he does ask to be forgiven if he has missed out any names so, in the absence of any recorded thanks to the police, I will accede to his request. In summary he adds how touched he was by the way that everybody rallied around at his time of need, and I suppose this incident vividly illustrates the value of close-knit communities and the manner in which they come together at the time of need.

What happened to the *Sanu* in the immediate aftermath of her sinking? I believe she was eventually taken to Town Beach on St Mary's for an extensive overhaul and then on to Penzance for repairs.

In recent research I have ascertained that the MFV *Sanu* was one of fifty supply vessels built in 1942 for the Admiralty; she was built in Looe, Cornwall, on the lines of an MFV (motor fishing vessel). But she was to come to an untimely and final end when, in 2001, while sailing along the North Cornwall coast, bound for dry dock near Bristol for a long-overdue restoration, she sadly suffered engine failure and her owners were forced to take shelter in the Gannel Estuary near Newquay. A lack of engine power and high spring tides caused the *Sanu* to wash up on the estuary, where she remained until 2012. There were many attempts to restore the ship, but with such bad damage it proved impossible.

The MFV *Sanu* was eventually broken up with some of the timbers featuring on a TV programme entitled *Do You Like My Grand Design?* hosted by Kevin McCloud, who built a clifftop shack on the Somerset coastline out of recycled junk. The shack's wooden veranda that jutted out over the sea like a ship's prow was apparently made from timbers from the MFV *Sanu*. This was a fitting end to a remarkable vessel that had provided me with one of my most interesting and unique crimes to investigate and bring to a successful conclusion.

In a *Scillonian Magazine*, published after the court case, it was said, 'and so another wrecking tale takes its place in Scillonian history!' The Isles of Scilly had seen many a shipwreck in its time, but never one like the *Sanu*.

CHAPTER 9

LEISURE TIME

My rest days were mainly spent on the islands. It was too expensive and the mode of transport to the mainland too unreliable – fog, rough seas, etc. – to nip home to Newquay for a couple of days, and anyway I enjoyed my life on the islands.

I did, however, return home after only being on St Mary's for two weeks or so and I am glad I did. I spent an enjoyable weekend with my father, who sadly and unexpectedly passed away on the Sunday night in his sleep. He was so proud of what my sister and I had achieved and had spent his last day typically carrying out a St John Ambulance duty. On his return home that day we had supper together with my Aunty Gwen, and a police colleague, John Burrow, made an unexpected call for a cup of tea having commenced a night shift at Newquay Police Station. Dad and I even had a bit of a 'tussle' to determine who would take the Sunday newspaper to read in bed – Dad won!

Looking back he must have found it very difficult to bring up two teenage children on his own, and at a very important time of their development, and at the same time come to terms with the fact he had lost, in a most untimely way, his life partner, love of his life and best friend. He did get a lot of support from members of our family, in particular an Aunty Edie from my mother's side and his half-sister Aunty Gwen, who was a spinster and who had forged a successful nursing career in Liverpool. Aunty Gwen retired from nursing and moved down to Newquay to live with us and she proved to be a great support to us all, even though it must have presented her with a great challenge coming from a spinster life and having a ready-made family to look after. She coped extremely well and became an integral part of our lives; and I am sure the same applied to her.

It was very difficult to go back to St Mary's after my father's funeral, but life had to go on and I had a very rewarding career that would distract my mind from some of the sadness. My Scillonian friends were most supportive and understanding, and this helped a lot.

I can't recall going home many more times before the end of my secondment although I do vividly remember a day visit to St Mary's by my grandmother on my mother's side, Nanny Whitting, who was well into her seventies, together with my sister Pauline and her boyfriend Roger Pearce, who was a policemen in the Metropolitan Police in London. Roger had been a policeman for twelve months less than I and he had met Pauline at a nurse's party, where a lot of policemen meet their girlfriends. He and Pauline arrived on the *Scillonian* and I was on the quay in full uniform to greet them. I felt proud as Punch. From where I was standing I could see my grandmother's beaming face on the deck that said, "That's my boy!'

I believe we may have had lunch in the Sunset Restaurant on St Mary's quay, after which I took them all on a tour of St Mary's in Joyce Pim's car – I had a car of my own by now that was garaged on the mainland and so I knew I was covered by my insurance. During the trip Roger inquired of me if he could ask a question and after my curiosity got the better of me I agreed. He then rather gallantly and in a most chivalrous manner said that he wished to marry Pauline, and that he rather hoped I might give my consent. There was always, and I suspect still is, a bit of rivalry between county police forces and the Met and after I had given them my blessing I said to Roger, "Typical Met – you have come all this way to ask me that when you could have used a telephone; we have got access to them here, you know." Roger, I hope, accepted this remark as good old-fashioned banter; either way he had secured the hand of my lovely sister in marriage and they have lived happily ever after. They proved to be a good catch for each other – it must have been because of my blessing and the Scillonian air!

My sister and I were always pretty close and the untimely death of our parents cemented that relationship even more. Our father, Bill, had a wicked sense of humour and I am sure that this is one attribute that he passed on to me. It did, however, backfire on me one day when my sister persuaded me, as the story goes, to swallow a torch bulb! I can't really be absolutely sure now if I did swallow a torch bulb or not, but if it was bravado then it certainly rebounded on me because I was taken to the local doctor and prescribed cotton-wool sandwiches! I cannot even be sure now if that is true either, but it does provide substance for a good story over a pint with friends or with the nieces/nephews and grandchildren, and of course going to the bathroom at night had certain advantages.

Boating and fishing filled much of my spare time – I just loved being out on the water and feeling the sun and breeze on my face. I wasn't, however, a good sailor, and on occasions had to fight extremely hard not to embarrass myself – I would never have lived it down.

Boating became my hobby – after my job I hasten to add – and my connection with my boatmen friends prospered. I even made a friend of the captain and first mate of the *Queen of the Isles*, which used to more often than not spend the weekend on Scilly after the late Saturday run from Penzance. The *Queen of the Isles* and the *Scillonian* ran in tandem from the mainland during the busy summer season. I would often pop on board for a chat and a cup of char, and learnt, on one occasion, how to cook a mackerel Dutch-style – I will include this in my recipe book to follow.

Some weekends Dai Davies, the captain of the *Queen of the Isles*, used to commandeer the launch that belonged to the Isles of Scilly Steamship Company (the owners of both ferries) and take her out for a spot of fishing. I was invited to join both him and the first mate, Len Skewes, but had to bring some beer and pasties – I never go very far without a pasty! On one occasion we were joined by a couple of young German girls on holiday who didn't actually speak much English. They thought, for example, that mackerel were called 'big buggers' because this is what we called them when bringing the larger ones on board! This was repeated many a time in the pub, much to the glee of the locals.

One of the girls was called Helga, and Dai was to publicly embarrass me on the day of her departure.

I walked to the quay, as usual, to see the *Queen of the Isles* off. I was in full uniform and the quay was full of tourists and locals who either worked there or were seeing friends off. As I neared the ship I saw Helga on the bridge of the boat with Dai, who handed her a microphone. After what seemed an age the microphone came to life only for me to hear Helga's voice saying, "Roger, I love you. I will miss you. I see you again." Well, if I could have crawled into a hole I would have done so. I bet there was nobody on that quay who didn't know who 'Roger' was – I was sticking out like a sore thumb, being in full uniform and blushing! Later that week I was to receive a postcard from London with a picture of a London bobby on the front. On the back were the words 'Roger. I am sorry – Helga'. I have never seen or heard from Helga since and probably that is a good thing as I am now happily married, but I often wonder if she still recalls this time of her life.

On another occasion, a lovely summer's day, Dai Davies persuaded me to take a trip to Penzance on the *Queen of the Isles*; it was to return to St Mary's by about mid-afternoon, well in time for my evening shift. I think all three of us were working that day and I had volunteered for the evening shift. I took my position up on the bridge and sat back to enjoy my leisurely cruise to Penzance, even joining the crew for a spot of lunch as we neared Penzance. Even though it was a fairly calm sea I didn't stay down below deck for too long as the smell of the diesel was beginning to turn my stomach – I could never have pursued a career in the navy!

Once at Penzance and safely moored up I set off towards the town to do a bit of shopping and maybe catch up with the odd friend or two that I had made while stationed there.

Yet I had not got more than fifty yards or so down the quay when I heard Dai hailing me from the bridge. He told me that he had just been advised that the *Queen of the Isles* would not now be returning to St Mary's and while apologising profusely had a smile on his face that reached from ear to ear! I suppose I could have telephoned Barry and asked for the day off, but being young and keen found my way to the heliport at Eastern Green and paid for a trip back to St Mary's so as to be back there in time to begin work. What had begun as a free cruise turned out to be an expensive way of spending my leisure time.

To fill my leisure time I did many other things that young men of my age might do, including the imbibing of a beer or two or rum and shrub – when off duty, of course. I didn't let lock-ins become too large a part of my life especially when in uniform and walking around the islands.

I also did a bit of moonlighting at a time when police officers couldn't take other jobs even with permission. I believe they can now, job depending. I was asked to do a bit of cataloguing for a local auctioneer called Walter 'Fuzz' Groves, who had many other jobs besides auctioneering. I remember sitting in a Portakabin type of building on Porthmellon and listing a number of items that had come from a house clearance. This job certainly didn't make me rich, but it kept me out of mischief.

Fuzz Groves lived at Old Town in a house called 'Nowhere'; he was a colourful, ebullient and enigmatic character who at one time simultaneously held down thirteen jobs. He was, for example, an auctioneer, insurance agent, gun dealer, beach deckchair concessionaire, builder's merchant, estate-agent representative, bailiff, shipping company clerk, St Mary's Boatman's Association secretary and ticket clerk, national TV/newspaper correspondent and local press reporter.

Fuzz sadly died in 1976 and was buried at sea, two miles south of the Wingletang Ledge off St Agnes. Fuzz, a Bristol boy, came to the Isles of Scilly not long after the Second World War, where he found a place and people in tune with his character and where he was adopted as 'one of them'. This is one of my heartfelt aspirations – the Isles of Scilly, to me, are heaven on earth!

With bunting flying for her maiden journey the Queen of the Isles *lies at St Mary's in 1965 with* Scillonian II *behind about to sail.*

CHAPTER 10

TRAFFIC: VEHICULAR AND MARITIME

There were not a lot of motor cars on St Mary's when I was stationed there, and there was no legal necessity for them to have an MOT certificate. Motor taxation was only introduced in 1971 for the first time. By and large, therefore, cars were run into the ground, although we did have powers of persuasion, the Ways and Means Act, and the resolve to get the really bad ones off the road and suitably disposed of. This meant, in reality, the owners taking them to Deep Point at the back of St Mary's and pushing them off the cliff to Davy Jones's Locker down below. This is something that had apparently happened since time immemorial and not something that we overtly countenanced. 'Out of sight, out of mind' I guess was our doctrine. In this day and age such action would undoubtedly fall foul of many an environmental or – dare I say it? – European law.

It would seem that this practice continued well after I had left the islands and returned to the mainland. Towards the end of October 1977, according to an entry in the *Scillonian Magazine* of the time, St Mary's was abuzz with the news that a £4,000 council tractor had gone over the cliffs at Deep Point, plunging into the sea to mingle with the wreckage of cars dumped there over the years. It was apparently later recovered by a local diver, who used a flotation technique, and it was subsequently towed to St Mary's harbour – there was, I am sure, some sort of inquiry as to how this mishap occurred.

While being stationed at Camborne, and following the confirmation of my appointment as a constable, I was sent on a five-week police driving course at Devizes. The course was quite intensive and involved considerable classroom theory work, practical driving and intensive skidpan training. It wasn't all hard work, however, as we did visit a number of tourist spots on our practical drives, such as Winston Churchill's grave at St Martin's Church, Bladon, Oxfordshire, and HMS *Victory* at Portsmouth. At the conclusion of the course I returned home as a fully qualified police driver with all the necessary skills to be a traffic officer – my confidence to drive professionally had been boosted beyond measure. I was then, however, posted to the Isles of Scilly, where we had no police motor vehicle whatsoever!

I did, however, become very popular with some of my friends who were learning to drive. One was the sister of the girlfriend of one of our special constables, a guy called Johnny James, and the other the son of a gift-shop owner that sold knick-knacks, ice cream, sweets and so on. This latter friend was called John Bourdeaux and he was even then a bit of an entrepreneur – he is now known flippantly as 'The Professor' and boasts of holding an irreverent qualification of SFA (Camb.) – I am sure you can work this one out.

John has since become a potter of national and international repute who creates his work in a studio set in idyllic surroundings near Old Town and the airport. He is known by many of his colleagues as 'The Alchemist' and he creates an amazing range of glazes utilising many local minerals. For the past thirty years John has specialised in ceramics and sculpture.

But in 2007 he returned to his roots and began producing paintings in very much his own style, utilising real oxides for his colours, clay and natural driftwood salvaged from many beautiful bays and inlets around the islands. John, in his time, has also been a licensing magistrate on Scilly and a member of the Devon and Cornwall Police Authority.

I well remember John, although it was probably his dad, shelling out for a candyfloss machine that John couldn't wait to try. I was on uniform patrol one day, with either Barry or Roger, when he invited us to try one as we passed the rear door of the shop that was in a bit of an alleyway. We hadn't more than got it to our mouths when around the corner came a happy snappy holidaymaker who captured our candyfloss moment on camera. It was a good job we weren't in the social-media world that we are in today – our faces would have been splashed across the Internet, and who knows what trouble this might have caused – there would have been no way of sugar-coating it!

I did deal with a minor-injury accident on St Mary's quay one day. A hotel employee, driving the hotel's minivan, had collided with a visitor and inflicted very minor injuries. It was, therefore, reportable and I completed the necessary paperwork. The driver of the minivan wore glasses and there was some suggestion that his glasses were not of the appropriate magnification, and so we decided to carry out an eyesight test at the police station. This involved asking the driver to read a registration number plate at twenty-five yards both with his glasses and without. I believe he failed miserably and this formed part of my file that was eventually forwarded to Camborne.

It was subsequently decided to prosecute the driver and he was duly summoned to the local magistrates' court, where he pleaded not guilty. I can't remember for the life of me now whether he was found guilty or not and, if found guilty, what his punishment was. All's well that ends well, I guess, in that the holidaymaker he collided with did not sustain serious injuries, and the driver continued to drive for the hotel but with a little more caution perhaps. Having said that, the quay could be quite busy at times with visitors and locals alike thronging right throughout the entire thoroughfare, and nowadays some effort has been made to split, and restrict, motor vehicles especially and pedestrians by the introduction of a pedestrian walkway.

The local magistrates' court, from memory, sat every two months if there was a necessity to do so. I certainly recall attending twice, once for the eyesight case as above and the other, albeit a special court, for the MFV *Sanu* shipwrecking case.

There was another of my cases that went to court after I had left the islands and this concerned a bit of a family dispute on St Martin's – a tractor and passenger boat were at the core of it.

In late July 1966 a pleasure boat known as the *Darlwyne* sank off Dodman Point near Mevagissey; thirty-one men, women and children tragically lost their lives during adverse weather conditions when returning from a boat trip from Fowey back to Mylor. The *Darlwyne* had left Fowey heading for Falmouth with a south-westerly gale forecast and was never seen again. Despite a week-long massive air and sea search only the *Darlwyne*'s dinghy was found and a total of twelve bodies. You can well imagine that this had a knock-on effect on the monitoring of the number of passengers on boats that were licensed, and this certainly applied on Scilly. As I have already said, the St Mary's Boatmen's Association was pretty hot on complying with this legislation in any case – it was, after all, their livelihood. Even so we heightened our presence in this field and monitored passenger loads most carefully.

This disaster did, however, cause a certain amount of apprehension among the visitors to Scilly, especially those that used the pleasure launches. This concern was, however, short-lived as it soon became abundantly clear to all and sundry that we had a tight hand on the number of passengers embarking on the pleasure boats and this was made only too obvious by our regular attendance on the quay at all times of the day.

One day, following a telephone call to the police station from a local resident of St Martin's, Barry and I attended St Mary's quay to check on a particular St Martin's boat that was alleged to be overloaded. The information proved to be true and we had, therefore, to report the boat owner for breach of his Board of Trade licence.

Within a few days, another call was received at the police station to the effect that an under-age and unlicensed/uninsured youth was driving around St Martin's on a tractor and we duly investigated. It turned out to have been brought to our attention as a result of a family feud connected to the overloaded-boat incident.

This rather sad domestic and internal family squabble eventually resulted in all parties appearing before the local magistrates' court, where the decisions taken by the magistrates reflected the domestic nature of it. The young lad was fined £2 for each offence as was the owner of the tractor for having permitted the offences. It was said in their defence that they did not think the Road Traffic Act applied to the roads of St Martin's because they were constructed and maintained by the islanders and not by the state. This was refuted by the prosecution on the grounds that any place to which the public had access was either a road or a public place within the meaning of the Act. It was said that the fact that the roads were vested in the Duchy or maintainable by the inhabitants did not affect them for the purposes of the Road Traffic Act.

The boat owner was fined the maximum penalty of forty shillings, or £2. Decimalisation had been agreed to in 1966, but did not come into full effect until 1971, although some decimal coins were introduced between 1966 and 1971. The boat owner pleaded guilty to having conveyed eighteen passengers on his boat when he was only licensed for twelve. His boat actually had a capacity to carry twenty-six people, but his licence was provisional on the basis he had not taken a Board of Trade test.

Chief Inspector Peter Selwyn Hart from Camborne, our subdivisional commander at the time, who prosecuted the case, said that he hoped lessons might be learnt from this domestic saga which had been brought to the attention of the police more because of a family feud than from any regard for public duty on the part of the informant. He added that this sort of thing did not lead to good feeling in the islands and he hoped the bench would see fit to make some suitable comments that would put a stop to this kind of tale-telling. In summarising, the chairman of the bench, Mr Rodney Ward, commented, "We feel this really is more of a personal matter than any real desire to be public spirited on the part of the informant. We do not like families to be at war and we suggest that the sooner you bury your differences the happier you will be." And so came the end to a sorry and unfortunate saga in which a family feud had been 'hung out to dry', although hopefully lessons were learnt and hatchets buried.

Just before I left the Isles of Scilly there were some grumblings as regards traffic congestion in the centre of St Mary's and this did prompt the local council to take measures to restrict parking.

Painted 'No Parking' notices appeared all along Hugh Street, but I am not clear whether they were backed up by any official traffic order so as to enable legal enforcement. I do not remember having to take any action where illegal parking became an issue; maybe the odd offending motorist might have been asked to move on if an obstruction was likely. Many a resident of Hugh Town, I am sure, could not but see the humorous side of things as the council workmen painted the signs. I am told that Matt Lethbridge Senior, former coxswain of the lifeboat, in particular, stood by gravely watching proceedings, seaman's hat shoved back on his head. He undoubtedly recalled St Mary's and the Hugh Street of his boyhood – there were no 'Road Works Ahead' signs in those days.

Road maintenance was virtually non-existent, although I have found an entry in a *Scillonian Magazine* of the time where it was said that the council dustman had been trundling around the country roads of St Mary's filling in the numerous potholes with stones and tar, the latter from an ancient-looking watering can.

The surfaces of all main roads on St Mary's are now much improved. In August 2014 the Department of Transport announced a £10-million package to improve sea links between Cornwall and the Isles of Scilly, upgrade roads on the island and carry out ports repairs. The new funding included £7.3 million towards a £12.8-million scheme to improve harbour infrastructure at both St Mary's and Penzance and £1.8 million to repair and resurface public roads on the island. Since that date the majority of the local road network has been resurfaced as has the island's runway. The airport has also received a major makeover as have the runways at Land's End. A specialist hot asphalt plant was shipped to St Mary's and installed near Old Town and the airport thus saving taxpayers a significant amount of money – not quite a BOGOF (buy one, get one free), but most certainly a BOGOHP (buy one, get one half price)!

The harbour at St Mary's is also well on its way to having the pier extended and widened, along with the provision of new freight storage facilities and improved access for *Scillonian* passengers. How things have changed in fifty years!

Old Town Bay looking across to Peninnis Head, St Mary's.

Cars at the end of their lives have then to be disposed of. These awaiting tipping off the cliff at Deep Point are standing right beside an ancient grave, an area no doubt which some ancient native considered to be holy.

By 1967 in Hugh Town double yellow lines were seemed necessary, but it could not be done without an official Prohibition of Waiting Order, published in the London Gazette.

The council, caught up in the general euphoria, even introduced mainland road signs.

CHAPTER 11

NOTEWORTHY STORIES

One Sunday evening I was sitting in the office at the police station when the telephone rang. I answered it as "St Mary's Police Station – can I help you?" only to be spoken to by a man who I thought said he was called Smith. I was, however, soon brusquely corrected and told it was Commander Tom Dorrien-Smith, who of course I knew owned Tresco. I apologised profusely and asked what I could do for him. He told me that he had had an *Echinocactus grusonii* – which I later found out to be a large species of cactus – stolen from Tresco Abbey Gardens that day and that he wished the crime to be investigated. I explained that in my view such a crime did not warrant us hiring a boat to get across to Tresco that day, the St Mary's passenger boats having finished their trips for the day. How wrong I was! Commander Tom Dorrien-Smith demanded to know who could authorise such an expense and when I told him the superintendent at Camborne it was 'suggested' in very strong terms that I rang him!

You will know what comes next, I am sure! After a telephone call to the superintendent at Camborne, Roger Maddern and I were swiftly dispatched to Tresco in a hired boat that took us to New Grimsby quay. On arrival we were met by a man driving a tractor and trailer – there were no cars on Tresco – and then driven unceremoniously on the trailer to Tresco Abbey. Having met Commander Tom Dorrien-Smith, been shown the hole in the ground where the *Echinocactus grusonii* had been, and taken a half-page statement we returned by tractor and trailer to Old Grimsby, where we called in at the pub, the New Inn. It was there that we carried out an inquiry or two in relation to the dastardly deed over a couple of beers – a very convivial way to carry out a crime inquiry, I am sure you would agree. We were, in detective jargon, 'cultivating' (no pun intended) informants. Once our inquiries had been completed we returned to St Mary's in our hired boat and then went back to the police station to complete the necessary paperwork.

Quite early the next day we received another call from Commander Tom Dorrien-Smith to say the *Echinocactus grusonii* had been returned to its place of origin and all was well. Our inquiries had done the trick. There was no evidence of the culprit wishing to permanently deprive the owner of the cactus – it was accepted as being done as a prank – and the crime of the century was no longer on the books, having been deemed a 'no crime'!

Commander Tom Dorrien-Smith was the incumbent head of the family in 1966, and in some ways he ran the Tresco estate in what many at the time would have described as a feudal and regal manner. For example, when he was in residence in Tresco Abbey the family crested flag would fly from the parapet, as would a family crested ensign be flown on his boat when travelling among and to and from the islands. It's a little different now, it has to be said, and even motorised forms of transport such as golf buggies are permitted on Tresco.

While I am talking about our only real means of communication, the telephone – well, I am vaguely – I ought to say that at night you couldn't ring out direct, but had to go through the exchange that was manned more often than not by one gentleman whose name currently escapes me although I believe he may well have been called Eddie. To make a telephone call late at night, and I am talking here of after midnight, I suppose, you had to undergo a form of Spanish Inquisition as to the necessity of the call before he would connect you to the number you required. This meant that every time you wished to carry out a personal check on a stranger you had encountered at the force's Criminal Record Office, Bodmin, you had to promote and hard-sell your case or else he went back to sleep and left you on hold!

In the current climate we are all spoilt for choice with the many and varied forms of communication tools that are available to us. Social media is at the other end of the spectrum from what we had available to us on the Scillies, and aren't I pleased! In my opinion it is, despite having some uses, much over-utilised, and has become a form of amusement, entertainment and self-publication. That's just my view!

There were many other memorable instances that I can recall, and each and every one of them means something to me even after all these years. Boatmen, like most men, I guess (or at least I am told so!), admire a good-looking lady and like to ogle them (sorry, I don't mean to be sexist, but in 1966 this sort of language/innuendo was deemed acceptable, I am now ashamed to say) and 'take in the view', so to speak. One particular boatman who shall be nameless – OK, I will name him: Ben Badcock – had a penchant for cupping his hands and saying such things as "Saw a maid today – they were at least two or three pounds each" or whatever. And up to his sad passing quite recently he would still always greet me with cupped hands and utter a random weight in pounds – didn't have metric in those days!

I also remember one day creeping up behind a friend, Norman Discombe, who worked on St Mary's quay for his father-in-law, when he was ogling a good-looking lady further down the quay. I crept up behind him and said, "Got to be at least three pounds each!" at which point he nearly fell over the quay and into the harbour!

Another story that has often come back to haunt me was an occasion when I was aboard a pleasure boat returning from an 'off' island to St Mary's. Having disgorged our passengers, shotguns were produced from the cabin and potshots taken at some shags/cormorants – they all look the same to me – floating on the water. Shags/cormorants are medium-to-large aquatic birds that are most certainly now protected by the Wildlife and Countryside Act 1981. I am not so sure they were protected back in 1966, but I stand to be corrected.

Bill Pender was the boatman at the helm that day, and there isn't a visit to the islands that goes by that he doesn't remind me of that day! There was no relevant legislation discussed at police training college in those days, and in my mind the boatmen were making an attempt to scare the birds away from their crab and lobster pots which were in the vicinity. I am not even sure that any shags were dispatched 'in the making of this story' and I am absolutely sure that Bill Pender wouldn't have put me in a situation that might embarrass me in days and years to come. He was, and still is, too much of a gentleman to have done that!

When considering the ethics and morality of this story you have to remember that this all took place fifty years ago when we weren't inundated with a plethora of English and European legislation that seems to cater for all our actions, good or bad, and that in the minds of the boatmen they were merely protecting their living and livelihood. Most police forces now have a dedicated Wildlife and Countryside Officer – how things have changed!

One other memorable event – albeit quite sombre and sad, in fact – was the sudden death of a two-year-old girl on Tresco who had apparently, with her sister, eaten deadly nightshade berries. Her four-year-old sister survived. They were the daughters of one of the Tresco gardeners. Because of the seriousness of this matter we had to summon Dr Hocking, the Cornwall County Pathologist to St Mary's to carry out the post-mortem. This was a very sad time for the family especially, and all islanders tendered their deepest sympathy to the parents at this awful tragedy to their young daughter.

Following the girl's death every available resident on Tresco signed a petition and handed it to their three councillors asking them to press for resident nurses on the 'off' islands or two doctors on St Mary's. The petition emphasised that no reflection was intended on any particular person, but that a realistic view should be taken of the difficulties under which doctors and nurses on Scilly were compelled to work. The petition eventually found its way before the appropriate committee of the council; it did appreciate that there were many difficulties involved in providing medical services for the 'off' islands, but felt that some action needed to be taken to improve the position.

Sadly, the post-mortem that Dr Hocking performed found that nothing medically could have been done to save the little girl's life. Although I attended many a post-mortem in my time as a police officer – my first was very early on in my career at Penzance – this one particularly left an indelible mark in my memory. As a police officer you can become immune to tragic and heartbreaking incidents, and each officer, in my experience, deals with this in their own unique way. It is only after retirement that emotions tend to be liberated and now I tend to wear my heart on my sleeve.

To end on a lighter note, at some time during my stay on the islands (and I believe I missed it because of visiting my home in Newquay) there was a report of an earth tremor being felt by many Scillonians, although I never spoke to anybody who actually owned up to feeling it. I know that the 'earth moved for me' on many occasions while living on Scilly, but I am sure it wasn't brought about by an earth tremor – more like alcohol!

Tresco Abbey.

CHAPTER 12

END OF POSTING AND RETURN TO MAINLAND

All good things come to an end, so at the end of September 1966 I reluctantly returned to the mainland and was posted back to Camborne, where after a month or so I was allocated a CID course in London. I found it very strange to be back among the hustle and bustle of downtown Camborne, but I had plenty of company and many interesting and challenging jobs. I also had lodgings that, like Penzance, were like a home from home. Mr and Mrs Jewels – Len Jewels was a former police sergeant in the Cornwall Constabulary – had a son, Chris, who was also a serving police officer. He had joined the Cornwall Constabulary a month or so before me and I believe his police number was 93. Mrs Jewels served up plenty of wholesome homemade grub and was a dab hand at pasty making – I was back in heaven again! The only downside to these digs was the fact that my bedroom was at the rear and not only overlooked the rear garden, but also the main Penzance to Paddington railway line. Trains thundered past on a regular basis, with the accompanying noise interfering with my sleeping after a nightshift.

I did, however, miss the Isles of Scilly immensely and often drove down to Land's End to take a peek across the ocean at the islands in the distance. On one visit to Land's End a colleague and I were handsomely entertained by the bombing of the *Torrey Canyon*, a 974-foot (297-metre) tanker, which was carrying 100,000 tons of crude oil and which had hit Pollard's Rock in the Seven Stones Reef. The vessel almost immediately began to discharge its oil cargo and its impact on local beaches and seashores proved to be immense. Because of this the government took the decision to bomb it and set the spillage oil alight. A massive clean-up operation had to be put in place – a major disaster had been declared – and the overall cost must have run into many thousands of pounds. Attempts to use foam booms to contain the oil were of limited success due to their fragility in high seas, and bombing continued for two days before the *Torrey Canyon* finally sank. A catastrophic accident, but the bombing of the stricken vessel was spectacular. I believe that Harold Wilson, PM, watched the bombing of the *Torrey Canyon* from the coastguard tower on St Mary's; this was most probably one of the best vantage points and, therefore, befitting of the PM.

I did my CID course from January to March 1967 at the Metropolitan Police Detective Training School in Walton Street, Knightsbridge, London, with lodgings being provided in Hendon. It made quite a long commute each day by foot, bus and Tube, but was, nevertheless, most enjoyable. Had it been a month or so later I could have lodged with my newly married sister and her husband, who had been provided with married quarters in Regency Street, London, the CID training school having moved from Walton Street to Peel House, adjacent to their living quarters. Having said that, it might not have been fair for them, especially during the early stages of their nuptials.

At the successful completion of my CID course I returned to Camborne, taking up a position as an aide to the CID. I was embarking on a career in criminal investigation that was to eventually take me back to the Isles of Scilly in 1976, where I put my local knowledge to good use. I will speak of this later when I recount my association with the Stephen Menheniott murder.

I also became a member of the Cornwall Police Choir, which again would provide me with opportunities and good reason to return to the 'Fortunate Islands', on a regular basis. Having been appointed a detective constable in 1967, and moving to Liskeard, I eventually moved back to Truro, again as a detective constable. Here I married my first wife, Delia, a nurse, in 1968. Delia was a sister in the operating theatres at City Hospital, Truro, and what with her shifts and my erratic hours we didn't always spend as much time with each other as we might have liked. I did, however, take up golf while at Truro and usually played on a Sunday morning. I bought four irons, a driver and a putter from the golf professional at Budock Vean Golf Course, near Falmouth, and a budding Nick Faldo was born!

In 1972 I was promoted to uniformed sergeant at Truro, and Neal, our eldest son, was born. I thoroughly enjoyed my various roles as a uniformed sergeant, patrol and office, especially my prosecutor's role in the local magistrates' court. It was always said, by a mischievous colleague in CID, namely Roger Harvey, that I was the only prosecutor to lose a 'guilty' plea! This scurrilous statement is, however, far from the truth; on one memorable occasion I successfully prosecuted a 'not guilty' plea of a person for driving a car without due care and attention and also made my mark in the statute books by virtue of a stated case named 'Jacob v Garland' (circa 1975). It concerned a minor driving offence and my name just happened to be on the information document that had been lodged to raise the summons – fame or infamy, I know not what!

In 1974 I was moved to a detective-sergeant role at Truro, and in 1975 our youngest son, Carl, was born. Delia had given up work by now and I threw myself into my criminal-investigation role and worked many long hours.

As soon as the Torrey Canyon*'s back broke and the pollution became a serious problem the Home Secretary ordered an RAF unit from Lossiemouth to bomb the ship and set fire to the remaining oil in her tanks. A corridor from Land's End to Scilly was cleared of all shipping and the Sevenstones Lightship towed to a safe place. In Hugh Town, St Mary's, Wilfred Tonkin, the town crier, stumped around the streets crying, "Notice: the public must keep off all beaches today."*

CHAPTER 13

CORNWALL POLICE CHOIR VISITS TO THE ISLES OF SCILLY

To supplement my leisure time, in addition to family life and a bit of golf, I joined the Cornwall Police Choir, which for a while practised every Tuesday evening in the club room and bar at the rear of Truro Police Station – during my stay at Truro I was the police club treasurer. As a youngster I had sung in the church choir at St Michael's Church in Newquay – as did my sister and father – and, with a colleague and two members of Truro Cathedral Choir, also sang at a Royal School of Church Music Festival Service at St Paul's Cathedral in London. I also attended a couple of chorister courses at King's College, Taunton.

The police choir eventually, however, moved to rehearse at John Keay House, St Austell, the headquarters of the English China Clay Company. The choir gave regular concerts for charity throughout Cornwall, mainly on Saturday/Sunday evenings, and then, out of the blue, came the chance to visit the Isles of Scilly for a weekend of concerts. This normally occurred either just before or after the Easter period and it was most certainly a hectic and most enjoyable weekend.

We used to embark on the Scillonian on a Saturday morning, arriving on St Mary's just before lunch. Each member was allocated lodgings with a local family and I was fortunate to initially be billeted with John and Dot Ozard, who ran a small guest house in Buzza Street, near Porthcressa Beach. Dot was a Scillonian and John, I seem to recall, came from the Channel Islands; he had worked for the Ministry of Agriculture on Scilly and had also been, I believe, a taxi driver. I was again in a home-from-home scenario and our friendship was to continue until John and then Dot sadly passed away.

Incidentally, I learnt, in researching for this book, that in the vicinity of John and Dot's house was roughly the location where one of the first bombs dropped in the UK by the Germans at the beginning of the Second World War landed – it was one of many dropped on the Isles of Scilly, apparently, with several lives lost as a consequence. In fact, a lot more went on in and around the Isles of Scilly during both world wars than I was certainly aware of. Many a British ship disguised as a trawler prowled in and around the islands and beyond on the lookout for German submarines and suchlike and flying boats were based in the Tresco Channel during the First World War. A number of contemporary New England-style cottages for rent are now situated on the site of the former Tresco flying-boat station, which is located on the western side of the island with associated spa, store, delicatessen, restaurant, bicycle hire and Island Office nearby.

I spent several holidays on the Isles of Scilly with Delia and the children while staying with John and Dot, and on occasions they would come to stay with us during the autumn after their busy summer season. We had moved to Barnstaple by then, where I had been posted, on promotion to traffic inspector – a strange move in a way since I was, at that time, CID through and through. I didn't spend too long on traffic, however, moving back to the role of North Devon's detective inspector after twelve to eighteen months.

The choir gave a concert in the St Mary's Town Hall on the Saturday night, the chapel on St Martin's on Sunday afternoon – followed by a singsong around the rock outside the chapel – and then in the Methodist chapel on St Mary's on the Sunday evening. It must be said that although we sang our hearts out and worked very hard to put on a good show we did find time to relax and drink a pint or two of local ale. We enjoyed superb hospitality from the community and this, coupled with the fresh air and sun, made it a very enjoyable and pleasurable weekend.

A lot of the local arrangements regarding our choir's visits were made by Richard Lethbridge, another larger-than-life character, who had been a boatman when I worked there. He went on to run the local haulage company.

There was one fraught police choir visit that oddly enough involved travelling to Scilly from Penzance in a force-8/9 gale on the *Scillonian*. Dai Davies was the skipper and he told me afterwards that had it not been the weekend for the choir's visit to the Scillies the sailing would have been cancelled. I thought that being up on the bridge would stand me in good stead – how wrong I was!

In the lee of Mousehole and the Cornish coastline down to Land's End all was fine, but off Land's End everything went downhill. We were being buffeted around so badly that the bow was going under the waves at the same time as the propellers at the rear were coming above the water and juddering the ship. All this was supplemented by a gentle and continuous rolling of the ship from port to starboard and back again. Dai could see that I was not enjoying the trip and suggested I sucked a mouthful of brown sugar – a sea sickness remedy that he assured me worked for his wife. How wrong he was! As I sucked the sugar I gradually found myself edging towards the side door of the bridge that was slightly ajar, and when I thought nobody was looking, endeavoured to surreptitiously and secretly vomit! This, I should have known, is an impossible thing to do, and Dai, realising my predicament, showed me to his cabin and invited me to rest on his bunk. I am pleased to say that the rocking and rolling of the ship did have the effect of sending me off to sleep so that when we arrived in St Mary's, and having washed my face and generally refreshed myself, I left the ship as though nothing had happened. This certainly wasn't the case for many of my choir colleagues, one of whom I saw carrying his false teeth in a sick bag! The *Scillonian* had also not arrived unscathed. Some portholes had been damaged by the stormy seas and she had the look of having gone through fifteen rounds with the maritime equivalent of Muhammad Ali.

Having finally arrived a good time was had by all and the choir sang their socks off, probably as well as they ever had. We even had a smooth crossing home to the mainland on the Monday, to everybody's delight.

Many a *Scillonian/Queen of the Isles* passenger arriving on St Mary's after a tortuous and rough journey from Penzance during my time there had often pleaded with me to recommend a smoother way home. All I could do, unfortunately, was to direct them to Morley's shop in Hugh Town, where bookings for the helicopter could be made (but only if they had seats available). It is often the case, however, that the return journey by boat to Penzance from St Mary's is smoother than the outward journey, and so those who could not achieve a helicopter flight probably quite enjoyed their sail back to Penzance in the setting sun. I even took the boat home one day with my now wife, Gill, and we enjoyed the trip so much that we even managed to consume a pasty en route.

In researching for this book I have ascertained that the *Queen of the Isles* was built for the Isles of Scilly Steamship Company in 1964; she was designed to carry passengers and cargo between Penzance and the Isles of Scilly, complementing the service provided by the other company ship, the *Scillonian*. After running her for the service between Penzance and Scilly from 1964 to 1966, the Isles of Scilly Steamship Company put the *Queen of the Isles* on a range of brief charters before selling her in 1970.

From 1970 to 1982 she operated as *Olovaha* in Tonga and from 1982 to 1987 as *Gulf Explorer*, a casino ship in Australian waters. She was renamed *Queen of the Isles II* in 1987 when cruising off the Great Barrier Reef. Renamed *Island Princess* in 1992 and *Western Queen* in 1994, she finally ran aground at Ranadi Beach, Honiara, in the Solomon Islands around 2001, where she remains to this day, rusting away. I recently found a very grainy picture of her final resting place on the Internet and, to be honest, it made very sad viewing – what a shame to end in this way!

CHAPTER 14

ISLES OF SCILLY POLICE
GOLFING WEEKENDS

In 1978 I moved to England, as the Cornish say – Barnstaple, in fact, which incidentally was the town of my birth. My father was in the RAF and was based at RAF Chivenor and my mother and he lived in a bedsit in Bicton Street. I was born in the former North Devon Infirmary on Taw Vale and because of this I have always claimed dual nationality, Cornish by parentage and English by birth. This came in handy at times; there were often occasions when being a Barumite came in handy, and of course in the company of the Cornish I was one of them. My Cornish status has been the source of much frivolity within my family, especially with my current wife, Gill, and my eldest son, Neal. Neal and Carl were both born at Treliske Hospital, Truro, and were, therefore, Cornish by birth, but moved to England when they were five years and three years old respectively. Secretly I believe they accept my Cornish status, but the subject never stays in the closet for too long.

I was, for example, allowed to wear a Cornish tartan kilt at my eldest son's wedding although unlike Neal I didn't go commando, as the saying goes – it was difficult enough just getting in and out of cars with dignity and it was especially breezy in the nether regions. I also, with some Cornish colleagues, wore a Cornish tartan bow tie with my officer's mess jacket at a Burns Night mess do at force headquarters and the Chief Constable, John Evans, liked it so much that we had to supply him with one!

For a while I kept up my association with the Cornwall Police

Choir, travelling back to Cornwall for concerts. I was also a member of the Cornwall Police Choir Quartet, and we also sang at concerts given by the Devon and Cornwall Constabulary's police band throughout Devon and Cornwall. We even found time to make a tape recording of our music (very old-fashioned nowadays, of course), and won the Male Four Part Harmony section at the Cornwall Music Festival in Truro singing a song called 'Meerschaum Pipe'.

Not long after my arrival in North Devon I continued my pursuit of golf at Ilfracombe Golf Club and later, with others, formed a North Devon Police Golf Society. I was its inaugural secretary and my duties included arranging fixtures. By then I had become a member at Saunton Golf Club. We played numerous friendly matches in and around North Devon, stretching on occasions to Minehead in Somerset and Bude in Cornwall. For the purpose of a corporate identity we commissioned a North Devon Police Golfing Society (NDPGS) tie that was made up of crossed golf clubs over the coats of arms of the main towns in North Devon, namely Barnstaple, Bideford, Ilfracombe and Okehampton. We used to present one of these ties to the captains of opposing male sides, including the North Devon Magistrates, although it did come as quite a shock one day when the chairman of the local magistrates wore his NDPGS tie in court – not exactly a show of impartiality! On the grounds of fairness and equality we also commissioned a number of pottery trinket bowls with the NDPGS logo on the lid for the ladies' captains.

In due course it was decided to organise a golf tour to Cornwall. This proved extremely successful and it wasn't too long before I decided to put together an itinerary for a similar venture to the Isles of Scilly, which has a superb nine-hole (eighteen tees) course on St Mary's. Many times since I have wished that I had taken up playing golf when stationed on the Scillies, but then if I had I would have missed all the boating and fishing.

Our first trip to Scilly involved around twelve of us and we flew by the then Skybus plane from Land's End Airport, where at that time they used bathroom scales to weigh you before getting on the plane – it is much more sophisticated now. We played matches against the ladies' and men's sections and socialised thereafter over a meal and a few drinks in a clubhouse that probably has the best vista on the islands. You can see nearly every major landmark and most of the other islands from the clubhouse. I had often joked that when retired I would take on the role of the steward at the St Mary's golf club. Mind you, I also said I might end up as a deckchair attendant on Bondi Beach in Australia and although I have been there since (twice, in fact), I didn't look for a job.

In our spare time there were the usual hostelries to frequent and I did arrange the odd boat/fishing trip or two for the more hardy members of our group. Guthrie Pender was more often than not our boatman and he, as ever, amused my colleagues with his inimitable wit and humour (assuming, of course, that they understood him in the first place). Sometimes we were joined by a few locals that I knew, one being John Dart, who was the licensee of the Mermaid Inn. John had coincidentally gone to the same school as me at Newquay (he was in my sister's year, in fact), and we were able to reminisce of times gone by.

I well recall one trip when John Dart was on board, and that was a trip to the east of St Agnes on a glorious Monday morning, the day we were due to return to the mainland. During the trip we spotted plumes of black smoke rising over St Mary's near the harbour, and it became our topic of conversation as to where it was emanating from. I believe at one time the Mermaid Inn was mentioned as a possibility, but only with a view to winding John up. It was, however, soon to prove not to be a wind-up as a radio message was received by Guthrie to the effect that the workman laying a new roof surface on the Mermaid Inn had managed to catch it alight and this was the cause of the smoke. John was not amused, and after what seemed ages a speedboat of some description was dispatched to collect John with Guthrie heading back towards St Mary's to shorten the journey. Fortunately all proved to be well; the fire was soon brought under control, the pub was saved and John's stress levels could return to normal.

I also made a couple of other golfing trips back to St Mary's with a close friend of mine, Ricky Ryle, who is sadly no longer with us. On one occasion I managed to secure the use of the single quarters at the new police station in Garrison Lane – (the old one had long been sold). This made a great bolt-hole to keep our gear in and sleep in at night, but beyond that we were either golfing, boating or walking and imbibing the odd tipple or two! We did manage to play a couple of matches over each weekend. Peggy Discombe, the wife of Norman (whom I have already referred to), organised for us to play against her and a friend, Pam Caldwell, and on the other day we played against Norman and one of his close friends. They were very friendly matches, albeit competitive, yet ending, as ever, in a most convivial manner in the clubhouse over a glass of wine.

One of the local golfers I well remember was Michael Hicks, who ran the *Sea King* pleasure boat in my day – he went on to become a local councillor and eventually led the council through a couple of periods of very choppy water as their chairman. Sadly, Michael is no longer with us.

Bryher in vicinity of Hell Bay Hotel and Stinking Porth.

*Rough seas during winter gales near the Mermaid Inn, St Mary's –
provided by Joe Pender and taken by Dave Sherris.*

St Mary's harbour from lifeboat slipway showing Scillonian *at berth with Tresco and Bryher in the background.*

St Mary's harbour looking towards Porthloo and Porthmellon from Garrison Gate.

St Mary's harbour looking towards Carn Morval Point, golf club and Telegraph from Garrison Gate.

Joe Pender and his dog, Bella, aboard Sapphire.

Part of a large school of dolphins (approx. 500) near North West Passage/Broad Sound – taken by Joe Pender.

Puffin in flight – taken by Joe Pender.

*St Mary's harbour taken from Old Quay looking towards rear of
The Atlantic Hotel and Town Beach.*

*Rainbow at sea in direction of St Agnes/Annet and Bishop Rock
Lighthouse, taken from Juliet's Garden, St Mary's.*

Scillonian *at berth in St Mary's harbour awaiting return trip to Penzance.*

St Mary's harbour taken from Old Quay looking towards lifeboat house, The Strand and Buzza Tower.

St Mary's Boatmen's Association launches gathering at St Mary's harbour to collect passengers and take them to the 'off' islands.

Sapphire *moored at Lower Quay, St Mary's, with the Mermaid Inn in the background.*

Garden of hotel now known as the Karma Hotel, Lower Town,
St Martin's, looking across to Tean and Tresco.

Bryher from Church Quay.

MFV Sanu *near Cromwell's Castle, Tresco, where it had been beached by the St Mary's lifeboat crew some of whom are pictured in the punt in the foreground – see Chapter 8.*

Sunset taken from Juliet's Garden, St Mary's, looking towards Bishop Rock Lighthouse.

Cromwell's Castle, near Castle Porth, Tresco.

St Mary's Quay showing former Sunset Restaurant, NHS Medical Launch and a number of 'off' island transport launches.

Sapphire *approaching New Grimsby, Tresco, to offload/collect passengers and return to St Mary's.*

The Seahorse *at Higher Town Quay, St Martin's, awaiting passengers to return to St Mary's.*

Beach at Higher Town, St Martin's, taken from the quay.

Cormorant consuming 'catch of the day', a wrasse – taken by Joe Pender.

Wild flower garden at New Grimsby, Tresco.

Flying Boat Club, New Grimsby, Tresco – see Chapter 13.

Round Island Lighthouse to the north of St Helen's – built in 1887, automated in 1987 and declared a Site of Special Scientific Interest (SSSI) in 1995.

Yacht Scabbard *in Belle Île harbour, Brittany, showing Roger climbing aboard, together with Detective Sergeant Ernst Gruber (brown shirt) and French magistrate – see Chapter 20.*

Cornwall Air Ambulance having landed on Samson to collect an injured holidaymaker; showing Joe Pender (in centre wearing shorts) and a nurse from St Mary's Hospital – see Chapter 17.

Juvenile gannet in flight – taken by Joe Pender.

Roger on promotion to chief inspector in 1991.

Leucistic puffin in flight – taken by Joe Pender.

Cromwell's Castle, Tresco, from Bryher – taken by Graham Andrews.

Roger and his wife, Gill, attending a royal garden party at Buckingham Palace in 1992.

CHAPTER 15

FAMILY HOLIDAYS

Delia and I and our two sons, Neal and Carl, made several holiday trips to the Isles of Scilly, staying each time with Dot and John Ozard. The boys enjoyed the boat trips, beautiful sandy beaches, swimming and crab/shrimp hunts in the Porthcressa Beach rock pools with John and walks around the various islands.

I have continued along this vein ever since, visiting the Isles of Scilly on a regular and annual basis with my current wife, Gill, and our dogs. Delia and I regrettably but amicably divorced in 1988, but have remained friends to this day. Gill and I married in October 1988. Gill was the process officer at Barnstaple Police Station, having moved down from Formby, Lancashire, in 1977. We have spent many self-catering holidays on St Agnes and St Mary's, sometimes with my sister, Pauline, and her husband, Roger, and on one occasion with my eldest son, Neal, his wife, Susannah, and son, Will. Will was probably too young to appreciate the islands, but maybe as a family – they have Imogen now as well – they will go back someday and enjoy what Neal and Carl experienced. Carl is also married now, to Caroline, and they have a son, Xander Lowen, the latter name being Cornish for glad or happy. I know they have often spoken of visiting the Isles of Scilly, where I am sure they would have a great time.

Although Gill and I did spend a couple of weekends in the flat of The Turk's Head on St Agnes, where John Dart and his wife, Pauline, formerly of the Mermaid Inn, were the resident hosts, we have always gone with our faithful dogs, who have travelled to the islands on Skybus. There was Sam and Oscar and now our current dog, Bryher. All were yellow Labradors and each had a distinct and enigmatic character. Sam (everybody's friend) and Oscar flew on Skybus approximately thirty times – from Land's End Airport to St Mary's and return – and Bryher has so far flown six times. Bryher, as you have probably guessed, is named after the island of Bryher. As he is a male dog we couldn't call him Agnes or Mary and the thought of calling him Tresco or Martin just didn't appeal to us. Could have called him Guthrie, I suppose!

On one occasion, Sam, Oscar, Gill and I were witnesses at a wedding held in the registry office overlooking Porthcressa Beach on St Mary's. We were getting some cash out of the cashpoint machine at Lloyds Bank in Hugh Town when we were approached by a man and woman. They asked if we were busy for ten minutes or so as they were looking for some witnesses for their impending wedding. We explained that we would be very happy to oblige, but that we had nowhere to put the dogs – in other words, we all came as a package! Before too long, we were standing in the registry office performing our civic duty and Sam and Oscar sat quietly at our feet as the ceremony progressed. You never know what you might be asked to do on Scilly.

Before moving on too far, I must make mention of one of our weekends at The Turk's Head on St Agnes. On the Sunday night we had ordered a carvery for our evening meal and were sitting in the bar area enjoying the odd noggin and soaking up the atmosphere – the bar wasn't that crowded, consisting mainly of locals – when I looked at one of the punters sitting near us and soon realised he looked and sounded very familiar. After collecting my thoughts, which necessitated me going to the gents to turn my pedal cycle around – those with a sharp sense of humour will know what I mean – I remembered the chap as being a former colleague called Brian Smith who had been the detective sergeant at Penzance when I was stationed there in 1963–1965. He had moved on to better and greater things thereafter and ended up, if I remember correctly, as a superintendent at the force's training school based at Middlemoor.

Having decided it was time for me to 'out' Brian, I looked at him and said, "Brian Smith?"

He, with a similar gaze at me, said, "John Hawkey?"

I said, "No, Roger Jacob."

John Hawkey had arrived after me in Penzance as a probationary constable and so at least Brian was on the right track. Obviously John had made more of a lasting impression on Brian than I had! We then spent the rest of the evening reminiscing of days gone by at Penzance and elsewhere – Gill had heard the stories many times before – and in order to do so a lock-in ensued! Not for Gill and me, of course (we were residents and exempt), although if I remember correctly I did buy the drinks outside permitted hours much to Brian's pleasure and delight. Brian was apparently staying on St Agnes with a friend, helping out with some decorating.

Lock-ins, as a matter of interest, haven't always been handled quite so leniently as in my time when the general public weren't disturbed or inconvenienced and a blind eye could be turned. In the early seventies, the local sergeant organised an after-hours raid on a St Mary's public house with the support of colleagues from the mainland, who were brought to the islands incognito. I am sure that this was only done as a last resort, although it did cause a few ripples among the licensing trade on the islands and especially at the time of the next visit of the police choir.

As far as I was aware, extensions were always applied for – at The Bishop and Wolf Public House, Hugh Town – and granted by the local magistrates court to cater for the police choir after their evening concerts on St Mary's and where a buffet was always supplied as part of the late extension. Even so, it did cause a bit of a fuss and I guess things have never been quite the same since. Maybe, in hindsight, we should have been more heavy-handed in our day, but discretion in those days was one of policing's better tools of the trade.

One major issue nowadays, in my view, is that incidents from the dark and distant past are looked at through standards and attitudes of today – this cannot be right. Hindsight is a wonderful thing, but it is not an exact science and the past should be left as the past, wherever possible. Learn from it, most certainly, as I have done all my life, but don't judge people through twenty-first-century eyes and viewpoints. There are obviously exceptions to this philosophy of mine and I would be the first to admit that – however, an open non-judgemental mind can be no bad thing.

There was also a time when Gill and I stayed on St Agnes with my sister and her husband when we bumped into one of my former chief constables, John Evans, who had by then retired – as had I – and was holidaying with his wife and some friends on St Mary's. We had popped down to The Turk's Head for a meal – as had John Evans, who had come across from St Mary's on the evening supper boat. What a small world we live in!

Gill and I now go twice a year, late May/early June and late September/early October. In May/June we stay in Hugh Town and in September/October at Juliet's Garden up by the golf club. It is a bit like going back home, to be honest. We both know so many people that we see as very good friends and it wouldn't take a lot to pick up sticks and move to St Mary's to live permanently. It is only the remoteness and lack of security as regards travel to and from the islands, especially in winter, that puts us off. Maybe if we win the lottery!

I also now have a tenuous link to the Scillies through my voluntary work within the St John Ambulance. I am currently the County Priory Group chairman and county president for Devon, and although my area of expertise and responsibility doesn't extend to the Scillies – I wish it did – I do keep in touch with the only St John member on the islands, Beryl Read. I vaguely knew of Beryl from numerous visits to the Scillies and met her recently when she was invested as a Member of the Order of St John at a ceremony in Clerkenwell, London, in 2014. I was present as a member of Priory Chapter, and I now meet up with her whenever I can and we share and discuss our love for our St John work. One of the busiest events she covers, with assistance from colleagues from Cornwall, is the annual World Pilot Gig Championships, when up to as many as 120 gigs, their crews and supporters descend on St Mary's from all over the world, mainly the UK and Europe, and race over a bank holiday weekend in May. It is quite a spectacle and a good time is had by all.

Pilot gigs were very much part of my life when a youngster in Newquay. They had been used commercially in Newquay Bay for pilchard fishing and once laid up were preserved and raced throughout the summer as entertainment for the tourists. We even took them out during grammar-school sports afternoons as part of our sporting curriculum, and what I remember especially was how heavy the oars were. Oddly enough, the gig I recall rowing in was called the *Bonnet*. She was green in colour and originated from the Isles of Scilly. It would appear there is very little known history about this particular gig apart from the fact she was recorded as being at a shipwreck in 1833, it is assumed in Scilly. Apparently her name came from an old lady on St Martin's who was supposed to give the crew good luck and strength in piloting by waving her bonnet from a hill. When she died the name became taboo for many years, with the islanders preferring to call the gig *The Old Hat*. It is also suspected by local historians that she may well have been used for smuggling trips to France.

In 1953, Tresco sold the *Bonnet* for £35 to the Newquay Rowing Club, who then undertook extensive repairs. In 1963, the year I joined the Cornwall Constabulary, the *Bonnet* was loaned back to the islanders for three years and she became the champion boat on Scilly for several years. This loan appears to have been extended, as in about 1974 the islands' gig-racing committee bought her back in exchange for a newly built gig, the *Active*, which was built by a St Mary's craftsman, Thomas Chudleigh. In her time the *Bonnet* has been variously owned by Bryher, St Martin's and Tresco.

There is one other story involving the St John Ambulance

and the Isles of Scilly. It occurred one day when Gill and I were hurriedly walking around the coastal footpath of St Mary's, having 'come ashore' for the day from our holiday accommodation on St Agnes. We had to get back to St Mary's quay by a certain time to get our launch, the *Spirit of St Agnes*, back to St Agnes. At one of the most inaccessible beaches to the rear of St Mary's and having negotiated a footpath through a tightly packed thicket of brambles and ferns, I espied a lone bathing-suited man looking in a rock pool. I immediately recognised him, despite his minimal attire, as a member of Redruth St John Ambulance Brigade, Michael Tangye, who was holidaying on St Mary's.

I called out, "Michael Tangye, what are you doing here?"

After a brief catch-up on all things St John, Gill and I continued on our tortuous journey back to St Mary's harbour. Gill is now getting used to me meeting up with former friends and colleagues in various nooks and crannies, especially throughout Cornwall.

Gig racing on Scilly showing the Bonnet.

Roger with Guthrie Pender aboard the Lily of Laguna *whilst on a police golfing weekend.*

103

CHAPTER 16

THE MENHENIOTT MURDER

In 1976 I returned to the Isles of Scilly as part of a team detailed to investigate a murder on St Mary's. I was a detective sergeant at the time based in Truro and my team leader was Detective Inspector John 'Chippy' Chapman. The local police sergeant on St Mary's at that time, Peter 'Robbie' Robinson, had been involved in an inquiry that subsequently uncovered the fact that a Stephen Richard Menheniott, an eighteen-year-old man with learning difficulties, had been murdered by his father, Thomas (Tom). The Menheniott family had moved to St Mary's from East Sussex in 1965, where they were known to social services. I do not recall coming across them during my posting in 1966.

This case was significant as not only was it a rare example of a murder on the islands, but it also called into question the way Stephen was dealt with by social services and led to questions in Parliament and an inquiry.

The Menheniott family lived at Holy Vale in the middle of St Mary's, and Robbie's inquiries led him to believe that Stephen's body lay in a shallow grave in California Field, part of Holy Vale, close to where the family lived. Once this information was gleaned, Detective Inspector Chippy Chapman, together with Detective Superintendent Den Lovell, travelled to St Mary's and supervised the preliminary inquiries, initial statement taking, examination of the suspected crime scenes, exhumation of the body and subsequent arrest of Stephen's father, Tom. Stephen's body was discovered buried exactly where Robbie had been led to believe, near the family cottage, with logs piled on top of it. It is likely that he died during the first week of 1976.

A team of investigative detectives was then pulled together and we all met up at the Penzance heliport to travel to St Mary's. Coincidentally, I was to find that Dot Ozard was booked on the same flight and so my local knowledge was proving its worth already.

It was a fairly open-and-shut case, although a picture needed to be built up on the family and their relationship with each other, especially between Stephen and his father and the occurrence that led up to his death and burial. We were on St Mary's for the best part of a working week and during that time there wasn't an awful amount of free time to pursue any leisure activities, although we did imbibe the odd beer or two in the evenings when debriefing following our day's work.

During the week I managed to find a number of local witnesses who could provide very useful evidence that was eventually used at Stephen's father's trial. I wasn't very popular with some, who initially didn't realise the implications of providing such evidence, although I am sure deep down they knew the worth and necessity of it. One witness, Willy Hall, who was well known to me as having been a docker on the quay during my time on St Mary's and who lived near the police station, spoke of having visited the Menheniott home at Holy Vale where Tom had, in the past, helped him to maintain his car. On this particular occasion the witness had seen Tom hit Stephen across the body with a piece of wood; on another occasion he spoke of having seen Stephen tethered outside the family cottage by a rope around his waist, the rope, six to eight feet in length, being tied to a glasshouse. It was said by this witness that in the thirty minutes he had spent at the house he had not seen Stephen move. Other witnesses gave similar stories that evidenced ill treatment of Stephen by his father, with one stating that Tom Menheniott 'did not treat the boy like a human being'.

There was one amusing story that I recall occurring during that week. During our inquiries we had to interview Stephen's siblings and at one such interview the subject of daffodils came up. One of Stephen's brothers convinced a colleague that his father did not grow only yellow daffodils on his farm, but also red ones. He even gave my colleague a number of 'red' daffodil bulbs, which he gladly took home to give to his wife. Needless to say, this was a wind-up and his 'red' bulbs turned out to be as yellow as they could be!

Our inquiries led us to draw up a picture of Stephen's life on St Mary's and of the lead-up to his untimely death. Few people visited the increasingly squalid cottage in Holy Vale where the family lived, and, apart from Tom, the Menheniotts were rarely seen around the island. When the community nurse visited to check up on the young children, she described Stephen as 'looking like a frightened rabbit', but did not see any signs of physical injury. However, in October 1975 Stephen visited the island's dentist, a Mr Barry Fairest, where it was found that three of his front teeth were broken beyond repair.

In 1976, Stephen disappeared. His family claimed that he had gone to the mainland to visit a girlfriend. However, the dentist, Mr Fairest, had been troubled by the injuries he had witnessed, and reported his concerns to the police. Our inquiries led us to conclude that Stephen had been assaulted by his father one evening at his home and that as a result he had died later that night in his bed. His sister, Liz, spoke of having witnessed the assault and of later finding Stephen in his bedroom, moaning and lying naked on the floor with his mouth bleeding. She added that she had checked on Stephen every hour until her father came to her bedroom at about 3 a.m. and said the boy was dead. Her father allegedly said, "Sorry, Liz, he can't have a funeral or a doctor," adding, "I have two choices, either to bury the body on the farm or put it over Deep Point into the sea."

It would seem that Tom Menheniott later enlisted his daughter, Liz, to help him carry Stephen's body out to his car. They then drove down to the packing sheds and from there took the body on a wheelbarrow to California Field, where Tom had already dug a grave in the swampy corner. Liz described how her father filled in the grave and then dragged a fallen tree trunk over it so that it would not be seen from a nearby nature trail. Liz said that she later planted some bulbs on the grave.

Thomas Menheniott was charged with murder, four counts of grievous bodily harm, and preventing an inquest by burying the body. He admitted the last charge, but denied the other five, and was committed for trial at Bodmin Crown Court. The trial began before Mr Justice Willis on 6th December 1977.

The prosecutor, David Owen-Thomas, QC, alleged that Tom beat his son over a period of years with high-tension cables, scaffolding, a shovel, a broomstick, a fence post, and a potato tray. He also threw a knife and hot tea at him and punched him. He was tethered outside the cottage and not allowed to leave. He had five fractures on four ribs, one of which was fractured twice within days of his death. When he died his father put his body in his car and took him to California Field, before putting it in a wheelbarrow, covering it with a tarpaulin, and taking it to the grave he had already dug.

Menheniott's defence to the charges of murder and grievous bodily harm was that Stephen had sustained his injuries having fallen out of a tree, but the Home Office pathologist, Dr Albert Hunt, in giving evidence, said this was most unlikely. It was his view, having carried out a post-mortem, that fractures to five of his ribs were as a result of at least four separate blows and not as a consequence of having fallen out of a tree. Dr Hunt said that in his view Stephen had died as a result of pneumonia and lack of oxygen in the blood stream, and that both causes of death could have arisen if one of the youth's lungs had been punctured by a broken rib. He added that Stephen's injuries were quite consistent with the sort of blows described by some of the prosecution witnesses. The defence did call two other pathologists to refute Dr Hunt's theories; they were Dr Hocking, the Cornwall County Pathologist, and Professor Keith Mant of Guy's Hospital, London.

The trial lasted nine days and on 16th December 1977 the jury of ten men and two women took almost four hours to return a guilty verdict on the murder charge, but were discharged from returning verdicts on the GBH charges. Tom was sentenced to life imprisonment for murder, plus five years to run concurrently for concealing the body. Tom Menheniott stood unmoved and expressionless in the dock as the sentence was given by the judge and showed no sign of emotion as the prison officers led him away.

The judge, at the conclusion of the trial, criticised Cornwall and East Sussex County Councils for their lack of supervision, although it was accepted by the later inquiry that Cornwall County Council had no legal obligation to provide services to the Isles of Scilly. Two inquiries were in fact held: on 20th December 1977 an internal inquiry in East Sussex County Council found that the council failed to properly supervise Stephen once he had gone to live with his father; and in January 1978 David Ennals, the Secretary of State for Social Services, instituted a departmental inquiry – this inquiry reported in September 1978. Basically it was determined, among other things, that the withdrawal of Cornwall County Council from the case was justifiable on both professional and statutory grounds and that the arrangement between East Sussex County Council and the Council of the Isles of Scilly for the latter to keep an eye on Stephen was too informal and ineffective.

And so came to an end a rather sad, gloomy and unwelcome period in the history of the Isles of Scilly. Could Stephen's life have been saved? Who knows? As I have said before, hindsight is a wonderful thing.

Stephen Menheniott's funeral took place at Old Town Church in July 1977. A representative congregation of islanders attended as did Sergeant Peter 'Robbie' Robinson, who was the senior police officer stationed on St Mary's and who was deeply involved in the initial inquiries concerning Stephen's murder and the discovery of his body. He was also officially representing senior CID and other police officers who visited Scilly in connection with the young man's death.

In researching this particularly sad tale I found a great deal of useful material in a book entitled *Death on the Isles of Scilly: The Grave in California Field*, written by John Purchas (solicitor), whom I was able to track down and speak to. The book chronicles this tragic story of brutality by a father (Tom Menheniott) upon his son (Stephen Menheniott), Stephen's ordeal on the farm at Holy Vale, the courtroom drama that followed his father's arrest and the official inquiry that followed, whereby social services were castigated for their failures in safeguarding Stephen's welfare. I am grateful to John Purchas for his assistance.

Tom Menheniott at Holy Vale on St Mary's.

Periglis Beach, St Agnes, which sits on the far side of St Agnes with just Annet and the Western Rocks between it and the coast of America.

The Turk's Head, St Agnes – Britain's most south-westerly pub.

CHAPTER 17

GUTHRIE PENDER

Guthrie Pender, as I have already said, was a legend in his own lifetime and I am honoured and privileged to have known him. He came from a very large family; he had eight brothers and six sisters. I knew his brothers, Bill, Frank and Gilbert, well and still catch up with Bill and Frank whenever I visit. Bill's wife, Nora, sadly now passed away, was a bundle of fun and always pulled my leg when I went into the paper shop where she was a fixture almost to the day she died. Bill, originally a boatman, went on to work on St Mary's quay as a docker and drove one of the forklift trucks. He is a great golfer and has been the Isles of Scilly Golf Club champion for many years – the sign of a misspent youth!

Guthrie was full of personality, although as age got the better of him he shied away from the limelight. He did spend the occasional night partaking in the odd rum or two, although he did move his allegiance to The Atlantic Hotel from the Mermaid Inn. Again he had a favourite seat, just inside the door, where he would hold court and entertain the visitors, many of whom frequented The Atlantic Hotel just because Guthrie was there.

One night when Gill and I were having a noggin or two with him in the Mermaid Inn, we were invited back to his house at Old Town for a nightcap. I sat in the front passenger seat of his van and Gill in the back with the dogs – I wouldn't get away with that now! On arrival he was proud to show us his greenhouse in his back garden, which was full of overrun and overgrown tomato plants that resembled a scene from *The Day of the Triffids*! There was no way you could get into the greenhouse to pick tomatoes, but it was most certainly a sight to behold.

In his sitting room Guthrie had his personal reclining seat, near which, at arm's length, was his TV remote control, his CB radio a bottle of Scotch and a glass. What else could a buccaneer want?

Guthrie was also very kind, although I did misinterpret a benevolent gesture of his one day that later caused me some embarrassment. When I went home to Newquay one weekend he gave me, I thought as a gift, some crabs to take with me only to advise me on my return that I owed him whatever was the going rate for crabs! I was mortified that I had assumed the crabs were a gift, but never fell for such a 'gift' again without offering to pay. Looking back, this was my fault for not asking, and of course Guthrie was kind in many other ways that cost nothing – his friendship and companionship, for example.

Guthrie was also very fond of animals; apart from his faithful dogs, he would often drive out to the duck ponds near Porthloo and Maypole and feed the ducks. He was also very partial to watercress that he would harvest from the pond near Maypole. I often accompanied him.

With hindsight, I guess that in policing terms I may have allowed myself to get too close to the community and certain individuals, such as Guthrie, but I was never placed in a situation when this worked against me – in many ways it worked for me as a person, in growing and maturing as a police officer, enabling me to provide a better service as a police officer for the benefit of the community. As I have said before, the community was my ears and eyes – my colleagues and I couldn't be everywhere at once and I could recount, and have recounted, many a story where this is truly exemplified.

In Guthrie's latter years he was extremely lucky to survive an aortic heart aneurysm that necessitated him being flown as an emergency to the mainland by helicopter from RNAS Culdrose. His life was saved and he returned to the islands larger than life, although he didn't tend to get out and about so much. He still, however, continued to provide a service to the St Mary's Boatmen's Association in that he monitored the number of passengers being dropped off on the 'off' islands so that pickups could be coordinated. He did this by way of a radio beside his armchair in his sitting room.

Guthrie now lives on in his son Joe. Joe lived with Guthrie even after getting married to Nicola and was instrumental in building an extension to Guthrie's house that, although originally a council house, was bought by Joe and Nicola after their marriage.

Joe took up where Guthrie left off and now runs a boat that is most probably, in my opinion, one of the best in the fleet of the St Mary's Boatmen's Association, the *Sapphire*. The *Sapphire* is a Kingfisher K50 passenger boat which was built to order about eight years ago in Falmouth by Kingfisher Boats. Joe Pender has been a member of St Mary's Boatmen's Association for at least fifteen years. Before purchasing the *Sapphire* he operated the *Lily of Laguna* for eight years, which was a forty-five-foot wooden passenger launch. Joe took over the *Lily of Laguna* from his father, Guthrie, who was a founder member of the association. It was the *Lily of the Laguna* that I spent a great deal of time on in 1966. She has now been converted into a boat that has her own modern-day living quarters and, following her conversion near St Just-in-Roseland, near St Mawes in Cornwall, was last heard of, according to Joe, travelling down the canals in France.

Joe was a member of the St Mary's lifeboat crew, having joined in 1992. I say *was* because he has just retired after twenty-three years. He made the decision to stop volunteering because of a lack of free time. The busiest time for the lifeboat is during the summer months, and this, of course, is Joe's busiest time for boating, his livelihood. One of the most spectacular rescues he was involved in was when the yacht *Barcarole* capsized off Porthcressa. I well remember seeing this on the local TV news and it certainly looked a bit on the hairy side. I believe the coxswain, Barry Bennett, received a bronze medal for his part in this rescue, which was also re-enacted on the BBC show *999*.

Joe has his father's keen sense of humour and sarcastic wit and can always be seen holding court among his boatmen colleagues, smiling and taking the proverbial mickey. He has inherited all of his father's navigational skills and could most probably pilot the *Sapphire* in and out of the islands with a blindfold on – and yes, I would be confident enough to accompany him.

Joe, much like his dad, is hardly ever seen without his faithful dog Bella, and if not driving his boat is tinkering at home with DIY, walking with his wife and Bella, or driving around St Mary's in his pride and joy, his Land Rover Defender. It is rumoured that one day he was actually seen riding a bicycle and to have seen him walk from his home to the quay is a collector's piece! I did recently see him walk across Town Beach, with his father-in-law, Ricky, from the direction of the chandler's but this proved to be the nearest place he could park his Defender to the quay.

Joe and his wife, Nicola, and their two daughters, Emily and Eliza, now live in Bill Pender's old house in Church Street, St Mary's, Bill having moved into a small extension adjacent a year or so ago. Joe has modernised the bungalow to a high standard as you might expect from a man with a multitude of skills and attributes. When I visit Scilly now I spend most of my time out and about with Joe on the *Sapphire*, to-ing and fro-ing among the 'off' islands with passengers or pollack/mackerel/shark fishing – a venture that Joe has specialised in over the last year or so as a means of diversification. All sharks caught, often in excess of 100 per annum, are tagged and returned to the water. Joe has also appeared in many wildlife TV programmes that have been filmed on Scilly while conveying the presenters and their camera crews in his beloved *Sapphire*.

Joe is also an expert in pelagic birds and has a fantastic collection of bird and wildlife photographs that he has captured with his top-of-the-range camera, telephoto lenses and various other gadgets that he is renowned for – I have a bit of a liking for gadgets as well, although I do struggle to keep up with Joe! Many of Joe's excellent wildlife pictures are displayed on his website and often appear in *Birdwatching*, the *Scillonian Magazine* and the local Wildlife Trust magazines.

I was very honoured a year or so ago to have my picture appear on his 'fishing/sharking' trip advertising board displayed on the quay. I was holding a large pollack fish – the weight of this fish got heavier the more times I told the story – which I had caught on one of Joe's renowned fishing trips. The picture did rather squash my head a little, but it was all done for a good reason; apparently the cost of displaying advertising boards was charged by size and by shrinking the picture he brought it into the lower bracket of charges.

The Isles of Scilly have, since my time in 1966, become a haven for birdwatchers, or twitchers. Twitchers are committed birdwatchers who travel long distances to see a new species just to add it their 'life list', 'year list' or whatever other list they call it. They even have their own vocabulary or set of jargon words that sets them apart from us mere mortals. Joe is well known to all the visiting and local twitchers, with many of them joining his shearwater evening trips at dusk in the summer as well as his daytime and evening fishing/sharking excursions, which extend many miles off the shores of Scilly. Joe will travel several nautical miles to catch up a trawler just to see which birds are following it to pick up the discarded fish. He also runs regular trips on Sunday afternoons in the summer taking Will Wagstaff – another renowned birder who lives on St Mary's – and his paying guests on birdwatching trips, normally taking in Samson, Tresco, Round Island Lighthouse and beyond so as to track down puffins (when in season), other seabirds and often the odd seal or two. On a recent trip we came across a large pod of dolphins, probably well in excess of 500 – this was truly a sight to behold.

Twitchers can be very single-minded – as can many of us, to be fair – and seem to take great exception to non-birders who just might stumble across them when stalking (if that is the right word) a target bird. Gill and I were walking our dogs, Sam and Oscar, through the wetlands between Old Town and Telegraph Road a year or so ago when we came across a large group of avid birders armed with a multitude of huge cameras and tripods and camouflaged from head to foot so that they might merge into the background. We were in our brightly coloured anoraks accompanied by two puffing and panting dogs and talking to each other; this behaviour was quite obviously not to their liking. We passed through them – the path was quite narrow – apologising as we moved along the pathway. It was abundantly clear, however, that they didn't really want to give up their observation points, which they guarded so covetously, and our progress was hindered as a consequence. We couldn't have felt more unwelcome or embarrassed. In fact, we later likened it to walking through their bedroom at a romantic moment or being in a church – each one to their own, I suppose.

A couple of years or so ago now I had one very interesting and notable trip with Joe, and that was an afternoon trip to the uninhabited island of Samson. It was our intention to disembark from the *Sapphire*, leaving Joe's crew mate, Kane, in charge, and have a wander around the island. I can recall vaguely visiting Samson many moons ago, and Joe had not done so since his schooldays. In my time with Guthrie it was necessary to drive the bow of the boat into the beach (tide dependent, of course) and then have passengers walk down a plank that was both narrow and precarious and not for the faint-hearted. In Joe's case, he moored the *Sapphire* a yard or so off the beach and the passengers were taken to the beach by a small rib, fitted with a small outboard engine, that we had towed behind us.

On one of the very first trips to the beach we noted that a lady had stumbled on the sand, fallen and remained in situ in obvious pain. She was initially tended to by her husband and some other visitors, but it became abundantly clear that all was not well. I decided it was time for me to put my first-aid skills to the test and was taken by rib to the foreshore.

A brief conversation revealed that the lady was in great pain in her lower back and we decided to make her comfortable in the position she lay in and to summon assistance. Joe initially rang the hospital on St Mary's, but was told that they could not respond unless he rang 999 first. It seemed rather bureaucratic to be honest, but needs must and Joe used his mobile to make the call. I said to him in jest, "What is the postcode here as they are bound to ask for it."

We weren't to be disappointed, and Joe almost laughed out loud in incredulity. His response was typical of his father Guthrie, "This is an uninhabited island with no postcode – what do you expect?" or words to that effect. The call handler eventually accepted the location as being near the island of Tresco – we weren't, however, that concerned as the Medical Launch based on St Mary's would know the location once it had been dispatched.

It was not long before we could see the Medical Launch on its way from St Mary's and, although the tide was receding and the channel was holding little water, we knew they would find a safe passage through.

On arrival the Medical Launch drove in onto the beach and a paramedic and nurse alighted. A thorough examination soon determined that it was not safe to move the lady onto the launch and the air ambulance based on the mainland at Newquay was called. In the meantime the lady was made more comfortable and strapped onto a stretcher.

Our next task was to ensure there was a safe landing place for the helicopter. The tide was now beginning to come in, but it was not threatening the spot where the lady lay. We first saw the air ambulance approaching across St Martin's and Tresco; it was a glorious sunny day and you could see for miles.

The lady was eventually loaded onto the helicopter, which took off to convey her to Treliske Hospital at Truro. The Medical Launch took her husband back to St Mary's – there was no room for him to travel on the chopper – and we began to load our passengers back onto the *Sapphire* for our return to St Mary's. We never did get that walk on Samson, but we did have a story to tell once we were back on St Mary's!

I am glad to report that the lady was back on St Mary's the following day to enjoy her holiday, and she and her husband made a particular point of seeking out Joe to thank him.

Joe's sister, Catherine, also has her own family and lives on St Mary's. Last time we visited she was working in the Town Hall for the local council and I have known her to wait on tables at a local restaurant. Both Joe and Catherine have inherited many of the mannerisms and characteristics of their father, Guthrie, as well as his work ethic – an ethic that is based around being laid-back and cool (to use a current-day phrase). Catherine and Joe are also shrewd, confident and extremely proud of where they were born. I was even corrected by Joe one day when I was recounting the vagaries of my Cornish birthright. I said something like "You must be proud of your Cornish birthright?' whereupon he promptly corrected me by saying, "I am not Cornish; I am Scillonian." It is abundantly clear that Joe and

Catherine, as well as being extremely proud of their Scillonian heritage, are always delighted when they hear anecdotal stories about their father. Guthrie would be very proud of them and of what they have achieved, there is no doubt.

Some might describe Guthrie as a likeable scallywag, and I can perhaps see where they are coming from. I can't help, however, but admire and revere his sense of humour, down-to-earth attitude towards life and positivity.

Some of the stories that abound in his regard might only be half true. It is alleged, for example, that Guthrie, in his formative years, stole some chickens from a local landowner and was duly summoned to court to be dealt with. It is reputed that the chairman of the bench was the landowner who owned the chickens – could this really be true? Anyway, there is no point in spoiling a good yarn. It is said that Guthrie pleaded guilty to the charge and was fined a sum of money, but couldn't afford to pay. To whom, therefore, did he go to borrow the money to pay the fine? You've got it – the magistrate-cum-landowner, who not only lost his chickens but also paid the fine and was never to see the money, or chickens, again. I am sure this can't be true, but it makes a good story.

Guthrie Pender and Roger outside Guthrie's infamous overgrown greenhouse.

CHAPTER 18

WHY A POLICE CAREER?

'Why did I become a police officer?' is a question I often ask myself. Whatever answer I come up with is fine by me as I wouldn't have changed my career choice for all the pasties in Cornwall – well, it makes a change from 'tea in China'! As a teenager, if I am honest, I always had somewhat of an inbuilt uneasiness of the police (not that I lived on the edge of criminal behaviour, I would hasten to add); maybe it was the authority, respect and general esteem they were held in within the community coupled with a strong moral upbringing that instilled in me an air of honesty and good behaviour.

Or was it because of an incident that occurred during my youth when my father caught me chalking on the wall of the TA drill hall in the lane behind our house? I was, as a result, unceremoniously sent to bed and read the riot act only to be made aware, a little while later, of a uniformed person who had called at our front door and been admitted into the house. My father later advised me that it had been a policeman – when in fact it was a uniformed St John Ambulance colleague – that had called about my chalking indiscretion. I am sure that this was done by my father in good faith to underline how foolish and antisocial I had been – it most certainly worked and I suppose I must have adopted the doctrine 'If you can't beat them, join them'!

I also knew many of the well-known police officers stationed in Newquay as not only did they well and truly integrate into society – the local Chief Inspector, John Osborne, for example, was a member of the St Michael's Church Choir that I belonged to – but they also forged a close working association with the local St John Ambulance division that was managed by my father, Bill. They used to attend to engage in first-aid training sessions, and of course we mixed with them when attending road traffic accidents and incidents of public disorder where our presence was required to administer first aid and/or transfer the casualties to hospital.

I may have also chosen a policing career (or vocation, as it was seen as in those days) because of my genetic and heredity connection – my great-grandfather, William Henry Beare, was Deputy Chief Constable (DCC) of the Cornwall Constabulary prior to his retirement, having joined the force on 3rd October 1864 – ninety-nine years before me. He was given the collar number of Constable 88. Oddly enough he was born in Devon – Tetcott, to be precise – so a question mark over nationality, especially a Cornish heritage, runs in the family genes! William Beare retired on 3rd September 1910 on a pension of £140, having been awarded the King's Police Medal in the King's Birthday Honours List of 1909. I did serve in two towns that he policed, namely Penzance and Truro, and almost Falmouth!

In a paper cutting that I possess in picture form from the *Falmouth Packet* (18th October 1902) my great-grandfather's promotion to Deputy Chief Constable is highlighted by the headline 'Superintendent Beare's Career: Police Work at Falmouth – Past and Present'. It refers to an interview given by my great-grandfather which in effect summarises his police career. It would seem as though William Beare was the first county police superintendent stationed at Falmouth, where he lived for five years prior to his promotion to DCC. He appears to have been a conscientious yet zealous officer who not only made enemies but also had many supporters. He was further described in the article as efficient, courteous and fearless and a skilful cross-examiner and prosecutor who could quote chapter and verse of the criminal law with the most learned of advocates. He also seems to have been a strong believer that all licensed innkeepers were personally responsible for the behaviour of their clientele while on their premises and not the police; this strong stance of his seems to have brought about a marked decrease in drunkenness in Falmouth – in fact, ninety-nine fewer cases over a three-year period.

It is said in the newspaper report that although things were a bit lax before his arrival as a superintendent, they had certainly not been since. It would seem he was a bit of a stickler for discipline and strict compliance with the letter of the law and that this led to a good deal of unpleasantness in some quarters.

Superintendent Beare had been stationed at Falmouth before as a young constable in the 1870s; he was later promoted to the rank of sergeant in 1876 and remained in Falmouth. In those days the Cornwall County Police had charge of only a portion of Falmouth, the borough being officered by its own force. However, the feeling between the county officers and Falmouth Borough Police officers was described as 'amicable'. This is not surprising in many ways as frequently each had to call upon the other for support, especially when the drunken seamen in port, many of them foreigners, became drunk and pugilistic.

William Beare talks in particular of his first Sunday in Falmouth as a constable when called to the Pilot Boat Inn on the quay, where a fight was in progress. He entered the pub with Inspector Middle and saw foreigners 'fisticuffing' while the landlord defended himself behind the bar with a poker. A desperate struggle appears to have ensued during which the foreigners produced their knives. Fortunately the locals assisted the police; one man apparently seized the crutch of a cripple, knocked down an Italian and drove several others over the quayside right into the water. Fights of this description were not unusual; my great-grandfather goes on to talk of another occasion when two Frenchmen set upon him with one brandishing a dagger. He goes on to say that he mastered them and locked both up. At that time there was only one inspector and five constables of the Cornwall Constabulary stationed at Falmouth.

Mine robberies were also a regular occurrence at the time; William Beare was dispatched to Camborne, where there was, as he describes, 'a deal of rough and nasty work to cope with in those days'. He had a hand in effecting some smart captures and eventually the depredations ceased. William Beare also had a hand in the investigation of a mysterious burglary in the area of St Erth. Everyone was baffled by this crime, but eventually the 'sagacious' young officer arrested an innocent-looking girl of fourteen years of age, and in the end she made a full admission of the crime, which involved breaking into, at night, a house and stealing money and jewellery from a bedroom where two adults were sleeping. At the time this affair and arrest caused quite a sensation and at the assizes the culprit was sent to a reformatory by the judge. What a change from sentencing nowadays!

Superintendent Beare was also involved in a murder case while stationed at St Columb. The murderer was a travelling tinker called Tommy Down and it took place at Cubert, near Newquay; Down killed, with a hammer, a companion and he was sentenced to twenty years penal servitude at Exeter Assizes because at the time Cornwall Assizes were not held regularly at Bodmin.

Wadebridge people also remember Superintendent Beare for his success in breaking up a band of poultry and sheep stealers who had plied their unlawful business with impunity for a long time.

Mr Beare, as the reporter describes him, has 'the honour and great credit of being the first member of the Cornwall Constabulary to rise from the ranks to the post of Deputy Chief Constable which is the highest position obtainable by members of the force'. The article concludes by adding, 'As DCC he will discard the uniform and his duties will largely consist of indoor work at Bodmin where a special residence is provided.'

The picture of this newspaper cutting is framed and hung with much pride on a wall in my home. In the same frame are two other pictures of him; one sitting on his horse-drawn carriage, which was one of his official modes of police transport, and the other with his family, including my grandmother on my father's side, stood outside the old Bodmin Police Station, where I had gone to join the Cornwall Constabulary back in 1963. He also rode on horseback, or at least I have another picture of him astride one and in full police dress uniform. I only ever reached such equine heights when holidaying in Argentina, and I am sure the horse that I rode was put out to grass after I had ridden it!

On reflection, my great-grandfather was better equipped for getting around his beat than I was when on the Isles of Scilly. However, I am not so sure that I would have taken to policing in his day when lawlessness was rife and respect for the law much less that it is today in some quarters. There is no doubt that he and his colleagues deserved every penny that they earned and my respect for them is immense.

Superintendent William H. Beare after his promotion to Deputy Chief Constable, 1902–1910, photographed outside his home at Bodmin Police Station.

Guthrie Pender on the Britannia – *provided by Joe Pender.*

Joe Pender at the wheel of the Sapphire *with 'Uncle' Bill Pender.*

CHAPTER 19

REFLECTIONS AND OTHER MEMORIES OF MY POLICE CAREER

I spent my career working throughout Devon and Cornwall; initially Penzance, then Camborne interspersed with my posting to the Isles of Scilly, Liskeard (CID), Truro (CID and uniform), North Devon (traffic and CID), Ilfracombe (uniform) and, lastly, at force headquarters at Middlemoor, Exeter, I worked in the Career Development Department, which included recruitment and selection for promotion and specialist posts. With this particular role also came the responsibility of being the force's Equal Opportunities Officer and all that that entailed; a 'poacher turned gamekeeper' comes to mind when I recall some of the irreverent stories recounted in this book. In all I spent thirty-two years as a police officer and retired as a substantive chief inspector/acting superintendent in 1995.

I was proud initially to have been a member of the Cornwall Constabulary that merged into the Devon and Cornwall Constabulary in 1967, linking in with Devon County and Plymouth and Exeter City Police Forces. In Cornwall we always called it the Cornwall and Devon Constabulary!

Unlike my great-grandfather, I never personally encountered a great deal of physical abuse while serving as a police officer although you were never very far from a potential flare-up even during the most unexpected situations – you always had to be on your guard. Often a calm yet firm and authoritative word was sufficient to cope with most dodgy scenarios.

I do recall, however, while a uniformed inspector at Ilfracombe, managing a serious disturbance at Woolacombe that resulted in the arrest of about twelve young men for an affray at a nightclub. Because they all denied being responsible it was necessary to hold a series of identity parades at Barnstaple Police Station over a bank holiday weekend. This not only made it extremely difficult to enlist suitable members of the public to stand in the parades, but was also a logistical nightmare, bearing in mind that we not only had twelve suspects to process but were in a position to call somewhere in the region of eighteen witnesses.

It was eventually agreed by the duty Crown prosecuting solicitor that it was impracticable and unrealistic to hold an identity parade per se and so began a process known as direct confrontation, where each suspect in turn was confronted by each witness. This procedure took me and a colleague, Inspector Cliff Wilson, something like fifteen hours to complete – in total we carried out approximately 216 direct confrontations, all necessitating the production of copious amounts of paperwork – supported by a number of colleague police officers who performed custodian and stewardship duties. I believe that this process, in its time, was one of the largest to have taken place in the Devon and Cornwall Police area and probably one of the most costly, bearing in mind we were all paid double time on a bank holiday.

From memory, this case was eventually discharged at the magistrates' court on the basis of cost and the uncertainty of how the evidence accrued from the direct confrontations – most suspects were picked out by many of the witnesses – might be construed at a trial with the balance of probability in favour of the accused person(s) being the order of the day. With hindsight, the right decision was unquestionably made; there were austerity measures even in those days.

Policing, I would suggest, is very much based on strict principles, rules, procedures, regulations and legislation, and this is fine as a starting point but not quite the answer if law, order, peace and tranquillity is to be totally upheld. Criminals and non-law-abiding people do not, unfortunately, sign up to the same principles of law and order and sometimes, therefore, the line between upholding the law, or not, needs to be somewhat blurred, especially by those charged with enforcing it. To make it absolutely clear, I am not advocating the commission of a criminal offence. I learnt this from a very early age in its most rudimentary form when I was taken on a night shift by a senior constable in Penzance to a local hostelry, where I was invited, in his words, to 'check the books'. This was a euphemism for drinking on duty and it was a first for me – in fact, it was my first taste of Scotch. From this form of 'informant cultivation' a wealth of criminal intelligence was derived and cases built against career criminals – I used this on many an occasion when a detective. We even received an allowance for such devious activity, although it wouldn't even pay for a pint of beer nowadays.

I also learnt that you had nothing to fear if a complaint was made against you and it was subsequently shown you were just doing your job. My first complaint occurred very early in my career while at Penzance. I stop-checked a young lad on night shift and, after taking details of his identity and reassuring myself he had not been up to any mischief, I let him go on his way. The following day his father called at Penzance Police Station to complain about my overzealous behaviour and I was subsequently seen by Chief Inspector Alfie Jenkins. Having ascertained the facts from my point of view, he smiled and said, "If complaints are made against you it is because you are just doing your job – if you had no complaints against you I would be more concerned." It was good advice that was to stand me in good stead.

I think most experienced police officers, past and present, would agree that criminals come in all shapes and sizes, from all walks of life, and that it is a small percentage of criminals who commit the biggest percentage of crimes, wherever that might be. I cut my teeth as a young police officer/detective on juvenile offenders, some of whom were extremely prolific, cunning and shrewd. As a young detective in Truro I well recall a youngster from a good family background who not only found time to commit a multitude of criminal offences, but also made it his duty to slip out of his house while we were interviewing him in the presence of a parent so as to let down one of my car tyres. We used our private cars in those days to get around and this one especially was my pride and joy – it was the first new car I ever owned.

I also recollect being 'done like a kipper' while we were visiting, on a regular basis, a young offender who lived on the outskirts of Truro, where there was some building going on in the immediate vicinity of his home that necessitated the digging of ditches, albeit they were clearly marked by posts. It was OK for the first visit or two as the layout of the land became familiar to me, but on one occasion, in the dark, I found that our dear young recidivist had surreptitiously shifted a post that ensured I reversed my car into a ditch on our departure – I wasn't that pleased, as you can well imagine, but at least he helped to push the car out of the ditch and back onto the road; the car was thankfully undamaged.

At Truro we also carried out quite a number of discreet undercover observations in some very odd places to detect offenders in the commission of their crimes. On one occasion a colleague and I kept watch on some car mechanics that were suspected of stealing petrol from customers' cars, only to eventually come up with the evidence to arrest them. During the course of the inquiries that followed we uncovered the fact they had also stolen petrol from my car when it had been in for a service a day or so before we commenced observations – I hadn't even realised!

A colleague and I also kept watch in a pub one night and caught, red-handed, a couple of young lads, who had booked in for a couple of nights, and were in the act of leaving without paying. They had rather stupidly written a note of apology the day before and left it in their room, where it had been seen by the landlord. We gave them quite a shock when we appeared out of the shadows at about 4 o'clock in the morning as they discreetly and surreptitiously wended their way out of the pub!

Another pleasurable stakeout involved attending a local good-class restaurant on the outskirts of Truro at closing time and remaining incognito within as it was believed somebody was entering the building at night. The lady proprietor insisted on feeding us first, often with steak and all the trimmings, and the consequence was that our work, if you could call it that, didn't commence until about 1or 2 a.m. Needless to say, we did not catch any prowler and I believe to this day that the lady just enjoyed our company. Oddly enough, I visited these premises on two occasions, once as a detective constable and then, three years later, as a detective sergeant, and on both occasions, when returning home during the early hours of the morning, had immediately to take my wife Delia to the local maternity hospital as the birth of both of our sons was imminent. The other odd coincidence, in a similar vein, was the arrest, while off duty, again three years apart, and while pushing my newly born sons around Truro city, of the selfsame elderly shoplifter – you couldn't make it up.

Prior to 1974, when the Police and Criminal Evidence Act (PACE) was introduced, the arrest, interrogation and detention of criminal suspects were that much more simple although there were, in my view, still plenty of safeguards/checks and balances in favour of any potential innocent persons. Pre PACE, it became a bit of a game between ourselves and the criminal to prove/ deny guilt or not as the case might be – mere suspicion was not enough – and it was accepted that sometimes one of us had to lose out, if only in the short term. Either way there were very rarely any hard feelings and often I have shaken the hand of a criminal I helped to put away on his release from prison or had a drink with him in a pub.

I only ever had two prisoners that tried to escape after arrest. One was on the way back to Truro Police Station on foot having been sentenced to a short term of imprisonment – he only got fifty yards or so away before being recaptured by a more fleet- of-foot colleague – and the other was a young man who ran from his home having been arrested for burglary, but who was recaptured almost immediately after a short but interesting chase. My uniformed colleague initially followed him on foot, me in my car, although I had to double back on foot before the escapee appeared in front of me and ran off in the direction of my car, which I had left with the engine running. Needless to say this spurred me on to keep running, and my colleague and I, together with the prisoner, finally collapsed into a heap right beside my car. I had visions of having to explain not only how the prisoner had escaped from us, but also how he had come to steal my car!

I well recall one visit to Bodmin Quarter Sessions, where I was the arresting officer of a lorry driver who had stolen a cooker off his lorry – although he was 'bang to rights' he decided to plead not guilty. The trial lasted about three days, during which time his defending barrister did his level best to rubbish the evidence against his client and in particular the police evidence. The jury was told in no uncertain terms that the police were the bad guys. Despite this a guilty decision was quickly reached by the jury and the guy was fined. I know he wasn't sent to prison because much to the surprise of the jurors he proceeded to help my colleague and I load the exhibit cooker back onto our police van, joined us for a cup of tea in the café opposite the court, where many of the jurors had gathered, and then bagged a lift home with us in the police van. The jurors were gobsmacked.

In my experience, each and every offender knew when it was time to put their hands up and admit their guilt; I even had one guy say to me, "Ding-dong!" when I advised him of the evidence against him and in conclusion added, "Does that ring a bell?" It's all very different now, isn't it? How often do we now hear the phrase "No comment" or read of instances of a smart solicitor/ barrister who has got a guilty offender off on a pure technicality of procedure – signs of the times, I guess.

Throughout my career technology in the police service moved slowly at first and then in leaps and bounds, especially towards the end; it proved most difficult for old soldiers like me to keep up. Very early during my time in Penzance, however, we had a spate of break-ins at one particular property on the seafront and it was not practical to lay on observations (mainly because of the lack of resources). But this small setback did not deter one of my more resourceful colleagues called John Carter. With permission he affixed a loudspeaker from an old radio to the telephone system at the premises in question so that any noises picked up by the handset, played through the speaker, could be amplified and heard by way of the police-station switchboard though an open line, paid for by the shop owner, I guess. I am pretty certain that no arrests materialised as a consequence of this piece of ingenuity, but it was most certainly ground-breaking for its time.

Later in my career, while a detective inspector in Barnstaple, we used, on many an occasion, the services provided by a regional Technical Support Unit (TSU) based at Almondsbury, and this proved marginally more successful. I recall placing a hidden CCTV in a small grocer's shop in Bideford by way of which evidence was gathered to detect theft and prosecute an offender; and similarly at Saunton Golf Club, where property was being stolen from the changing rooms. This latter site wasn't quite so successful in that we soon learnt that the CCTV needed to be monitored by officers in close vicinity as although an offender was detected committing thefts the image wasn't sufficiently clear to identity the perpetrator. We then tweaked our strategy and placed an officer in the roof space with a monitor, but this soon went awry when the officer put a foot though the ceiling and blew their cover – you can't win them all.

As a young detective it was your responsibility to basically see a case through from beginning to end, and this included on many occasions dusting for and lifting fingerprints at break-ins (they weren't called burglaries in those days; this was the term for breaking into a house at night), taking prisoners' fingerprints/photographs, file preparation and typing all court disposals. Most of our disposal paperwork was done in the evenings, but followed most fittingly by a pint or two afterwards cultivating informants. There was no such thing as taped interviews in those days, so as you can imagine there was quite a bit of paperwork to get through in one form or other. Before I retired, the police service was beginning to use computers and associated technology for any number of administrative and database functions. My last role meant that I had to master the use of emails, which at first I found strange, but now I wouldn't be without them.

I have numerous memories of incidents, small and complex, good and bad, that come to mind. Some I have already mentioned; others revolve around funny yet serious matters such as the time we had a young woman with learning difficulties report the theft of her pedal cycle only for us to find out it had been taken by some young men after they had allegedly raped her. There was also the time that I investigated a pure and simple anonymous threatening letter that resulted in me carrying out, with others, quite a major inquiry at a local hospital in regard to the theft of drugs while at the same time interviewing persons intimately involved with white magic, including the Bishop of Truro, who I hasten to add was not involved in the case in any way, shape or form. He was merely able to advise me as to how rife this sort of thing was in certain parts of Cornwall and of the possible connotation this pagan milieu had to my inquiry.

There was also an occasion when I was involved in organising a children's crime-prevention poster competition with the comedian Lenny Henry acting as the judge, taking him to lunch and then acting as a bearer at the funeral of a retired colleague immediately afterwards. You couldn't have done two more varied things in one day.

My two postings to Camborne weren't especially that memorable, apart from being allocated a period as aide to CID, where I cut my teeth on dealing with crime and had many dealings with the travelling community who lived at Carn Brea, Pool (between Camborne and Redruth), and being locked in the police station one night by padlock and chain during the Camborne School of Mines Rag Week. Fortunately we managed to find a bolt cutter in the garage workshop at the police station and nobody, as far as I know, was any the wiser. Liskeard was a similar non-event posting, albeit for only about six weeks, although it was memorable as my first posting as a substantive detective constable. I did, however, spend most of my time on administrative duties, recording crime. The force had recently introduced a computerised crime-recording system, but needless to say this did require quite a bit of inputting by a person who in this case was me.

Early in my career saw the advent of police dogs in the Cornwall Constabulary and, although there weren't that many, it did assist us as detectives, especially when we became versed in barking like a dog when confronting burglars on rooftops. We did this on one occasion I recall in Truro when Detective Sergeant Chippy Chapman barked and between us we talked an offender down from a roof. He was surprised to see no angry and vicious dog when he joined us, but was never the wiser.

What was the most rewarding part of my career apart from the Isles of Scilly? Well, Penzance was one place where I cut my teeth on policing and where working odd hours and shifts became part of my life and the norm for the next thirty-two years. Weekends were never the same again; for most of my career I worked three out of four weekends and more often than not worked most bank holidays, including Christmas.

My next most favourite and impressionable time was the period I spent in Truro both as a detective constable/sergeant/ acting detective inspector and as a uniformed sergeant (patrol, office and courts). It was the first time I fully appreciated the tangible worth of teamwork and team spirit and this abounded there in bucketloads. They even built a new police station around us during my time in Truro, but even that has been knocked down now. As a newly promoted uniformed sergeant I had the pleasure of working with a team of young and some not so young officers who gelled together into a great team, and we both worked hard and played hard. On our night-shift week each officer would provide the meal for one of the nights, more often than not a one-pot casserole or something similar, like a curry or chilli con carne – we even indulged in freshly cooked pasties on one night of the week and at Christmas a turkey roast was served up in two sittings, it has to be stressed, so that a presence was kept on the streets at all times. Two of the most regular jobs we had to deal with, on night shift especially, was attending County Hall to search through vehicle and driver records, and the accident and emergency department at City Hospital, Truro, to deal with breath tests on behalf of our colleagues throughout the county who were dealing with road accidents.

Finally, Ilfracombe, where I spent twenty-five per cent of my career, was another of my spiritual homes. The officers based there were all basically young, keen and driven. It was a breeding station for probationary police officers, who were posted there straight from training school. During my time at Ilfracombe some eighty-plus probationers came and went to pastures new and many went on to forge very successful careers within the force. Only two were posted elsewhere for reassessment and subsequently had their services dispensed with. I am very proud of that record.

Ilfracombe was a very busy station in any number of ways and, being somewhat isolated, we had to manage more often than not with the lean resources we had. Somehow it seemed to work and the best was brought out both in individuals and collectively as a team. As the deputy subdivisional commander, later commander, I embraced and encapsulated the camaraderie and inbred team spirit that abounded and formed, as a result, a Community Orientated Policing Team, or COP Team for short, combining all community constables within the subdivision ranging from Lynton to Combe Martin, Ilfracombe and Woolacombe. It seemed to work, and many successful projects were achieved throughout the entire patch. We also engaged in fundraising activities such as 'patrolling' the coastal footpath between the Devon/Somerset border and Woolacombe. It took us two days to complete the thirty-five-mile walk and we raised several thousands of pounds towards a local scanner appeal. We also did a twenty-five-mile walk in a single day around Exmoor and raised further monies for the scanner appeal.

We initiated a Crime Prevention Panel at Ilfracombe following a public meeting chaired by myself and the local detective inspector, Peter Casey. It was, from memory, one of the first to be formed in the force area and, remarkably, it is still in being today. We also investigated the use of CCTV as a crime-prevention measure and not long after my departure in 1991 it was introduced in the town – it is still in operation to this day.

When I was posted to Ilfracombe I, in effect, ended my CID career path and returned to uniform duties, although in my first three months at Ilfracombe I became the senior investigating officer for a major fire in the town, where the arcade was seriously damaged and one life was lost. I also managed a team of detectives on an inquiry into a serious affray between local factions that resulted in one person being stabbed and seriously injured; this inquiry included a visit to Leicester Prison to interview the injured party, who had been sent there for having committed other offences.

While at Ilfracombe the methodology of setting goals, objectives and a strategic action plan became fashionable and I, with my team of sergeants in conjunction with some more forward-thinking constables, drew up our plan and published it. It proved to be quite a hit when we received a visit from Her Majesty's Inspector of Constabularies, although I did worry a little as to how some of my rank-and-file colleagues would react to it when asked by the HMI. I needn't have worried because one of the more junior probationary constables chipped in and provided evidence of an in-depth knowledge of the initiative and went on to praise its worth – he is a chief superintendent now!

The camaraderie at Ilfracombe was helped by the fact we had a small yet intimate police club within the police station where we could socialise after work. It provided a very relaxing venue in which to unwind and where rank didn't particularly count. It was also great when the celebrities starring in the summertime shows in the town popped in for a drink – Frank Carson is one person that comes to mind, and his presence always ensured a good turnout. I had a game of golf with him once at Saunton, with others, and his humorous demeanour on the course was as effervescent and bubbly as he was on stage and TV. He was a

135

very benevolent and charitable man who did a lot for charity – what a cracker!

Lynton and Lynmouth were also part of my patch and I spent time there on a needs basis. It was very well managed by a most competent sergeant, Ken Crocker – later by an equally competent sergeant, Bob Lee – and a team of experienced police officers that always valued your support, yet with a keen sense of humour. I well remember visiting Lynton and Lynmouth as a young boy not long after the flood disaster; a very young PC Derek Harper was stationed there at the time of the floods and was awarded the George Medal for his bravery – he was an inquiry clerk at Ilfracombe throughout my time there. No such disasters took place during my time, thank goodness, although we did deal with a very serious bus accident as well as a search and protracted inquiry for a missing person who to this day, as far as I know, has not been found.

When I left Ilfracombe in 1991 I literally bawled all the way home as it felt as though I was leaving something very special – I was, but I was about to embark upon what became my final posting and challenge and for which I was excited yet somewhat apprehensive.

Working at police headquarters in Exeter was a complete new ball game to me – out in the sticks we often referred to it as Muddlemoor as opposed to Middlemoor, or the Kremlin, for well-meaning yet derogatory reasons. Well, the grass is always greener on the other, side isn't it? The first thing I found onerous was the fifty-five-mile commute to work each day (110 miles there and back), although I could more often than not complete the journey in about one hour using the North Devon link road and the M5 – Middlemoor is situated just off the M5. This potentially monotonous journey wasn't always the norm, thank goodness, as on occasions I would visit other venues in the force area and to do so used a pool vehicle.

I also found myself working closely with the senior management team, especially Brian Eastwood the Assistant Chief Constable (personnel) and on occasions the Chief Constable, John Evans. My direct line managers were Superintendent Pat

Grimley, who had worked with me at Barnstaple, and Mike Keatt, who was the department's chief superintendent – Mike was a former member of the Cornwall Constabulary. Although my prime function was in career development – developing, monitoring and managing a staff-appraisal system and advising officers on their career paths – I was also responsible for equal opportunities, police recruitment, and selection for promotion and specialist posts. This often necessitated my compiling and recommending a strategy and process that ensured uniformity, openness and fairness, and this did, on occasions, prove to be time-consuming and very frustrating. Consultation and associated processes seemed to take for ever, but eventually and after much bureaucracy selection processes/policies were agreed and activated.

I did attend a number of specialist courses that enabled me to do this work – primarily at the police staff college at Bramshill, but also at professional training providers who specialised in psychometric testing, including both verbal and numerical reasoning. This all seemed a little like psychobabble when I was first introduced to it, but once I got to accept that it was only a guide then it did make sense. I also attended many Home Office-run courses on equal opportunities and on one occasion had the pleasure of having my brother-in-law, Roger Pearce, representing the Metropolitan Police on the same course. We didn't know until we met at the venue – it was the first and only time we 'served' together.

I did enjoy my involvement with police recruitment, and in doing so met a wide variety of potential entrants. As a sign of the times my last recruitment board involved a cross-gender applicant that didn't faze me, but I know that some of my more mature and culturally entrenched colleagues weren't that keen to become involved. In the end the applicant withdrew from the process just prior to interview.

One of the other functions that fell to me was the organisation and running of long-service-medal presentation ceremonies on behalf of the Chief Constable. I enjoyed this role immensely as it provided me with an opportunity to catch up with former colleagues and their families that I had not seen for quite some time. I also arranged the annual Probationary and Community Constable of the Year Awards, which again were presided over by the Chief Constable.

I thoroughly enjoyed my four years at Middlemoor, although I did miss immensely the hands-on involvement with the public, dealing with everyday problems and working with a team of operational colleagues. It did give me, however, a magnificent insight into the philosophy and everyday workings of personnel management – or human resources, as they call it nowadays – together with the management of people and endeavouring to meet their expectations in regard to their career paths. Some it has to be said had a greater expectation than their abilities and this did present challenges – I like challenges!

Serving at force headquarters also enhanced my interpersonal and diplomacy skills and provided me with much confidence in working with officers of ACPO (Association of Chief Police Officers) rank and I learnt never to fear an interview. I certainly knew what to expect, having personally developed systems for selection based on job descriptions, person specification and both essential and desirable skills each supported by evidence of ability. In this regard I am pleased to say that I did pass my promotion board for selection to superintendent; and although I remained in the pool for promotion until the day I retired, I did end my days as an acting superintendent, which I guess was a bonus of sorts. I got the job, but not the pay; money isn't everything, after all.

This headquarters job of mine was, however, to prove to be my last in the police service and in early September 1995 I left Middlemoor with a heavy heart, but with fantastic and treasured memories of a long, varied and interesting police career. It would have been great to have ended my career back out in the sticks doing proper police work, but it wasn't to be. All good things have to come to an end, and with hindsight I guess that the wide variety of people and management skills that I learnt and mastered during my headquarters posting made me an even more rounded person. I was truly prepared and adequately equipped for what was to come in what I have always termed as the 'real world'.

In my case this was acting as the chief executive of Devon St John Ambulance for five years, where working with volunteers, and a pretty rudimentary human-resources environment presented its own inimitable confrontations and unparalleled challenges. This was followed by my role as clerk to Instow Parish Council for twelve and a half years, where to a degree a sense of structure and air of professionalism prevailed within the ambit of local government.

To a degree my role as clerk to Instow Parish Council fulfilled my desire and craving to serve the public at the 'coalface' yet again, albeit in a slightly different format to a police officer, although not really that far removed. It was somewhat akin to my community-policing role on the Isles of Scilly, although it didn't come with the same powers, uniform or salary; the principles were, however, the same and my police work ethic and background stood me in good stead.

CHAPTER 20

POLICING ON OTHER ISLANDS

My police career, besides taking me to the Isles of Scilly, has also enabled me to perform my various roles and duties in other island communities, both inside and well beyond the boundaries of Devon and Cornwall.

In the mid to late seventies I dealt with an extradition case while a detective sergeant at Truro. A yacht named the *Scabbard* was stolen from Penpol Creek near Truro and later traced, by way of Interpol, to an island off the south coast of Brittany – Belle Île. It was in the possession of two Austrian males, who were arrested by the French gendarmerie. Together with a member of the local Regional Crime Squad, Ernst Gruber – an Austrian national – a Scenes of Crime Officer, Trevor Hill, and a friend of the owner of the yacht, we travelled to Brittany, where the offenders were interviewed. We caught the overnight ferry from Plymouth to Roscoff and were then escorted down through Brittany by a couple of plain-clothes gendarmerie whose local knowledge proved most invaluable. They guided us to a place called La Trinité-sur-Mer, where we caught the ferry to Belle Île; they accompanied us.

A hastily convened court was arranged on the island at the police station and a preliminary extradition application made to a magistrate who had travelled from the mainland of Brittany to Belle Île. The two Austrian offenders were duly remanded in custody and subsequently moved to a prison in Paris to await an extradition request. In fact they travelled, under police escort, on the ferry to the mainland of Brittany the following day – we were on the same ferry.

It must have been quite an unusual occurrence for Belle Île as the magistrate travelled from the mainland of Brittany, accompanied by his wife and secretary, and insisted on wining and dining us at a local restaurant on Belle Île before we got to work. The meal, I well remember, consisted of oysters, fresh crab and a variety of other types of local seafood washed down by a glass or two of chilled white wine. I am pleased to say that we didn't overindulge as we knew we had work to do and the language barrier to overcome – the wine probably helped. We used a teacher who taught English at the island's school as an interpreter and although the offenders spoke perfect English Ernst insisted on taking down their admission statements in German – he needed to justify his presence!

After a successful extradition application I subsequently travelled to Paris with Ernst Gruber and Detective Inspector Chippy Chapman – rank has its privileges, after all – for the purpose of bringing the Austrian offenders back to the UK for trial. After an overnight stop in Paris at a small hotel run by an ex-Metropolitan Police officer in a road called Rue Jacob – you couldn't make it up – the party returned to the UK and the offenders were duly sentenced.

On both visits to France the language difference didn't cause us too much of a problem. I had a scant knowledge of French by virtue of a failed O level at school and the police lingo, procedure and sense of humour especially seemed to transcend any communication issues. Life for the gendarmerie on Belle Île was much the same as I had experienced on the Isles of Scilly, and we were able to share experiences and anecdotes with minimal difficulty. I guess that the Westcountry drawl was very similar to the way in which French was spoken in Brittany and this became markedly apparent when we travelled to Paris, where the French language was much more cultured. We did, however, come into difficulties one day in Paris after having lunch at a pavement café and requesting a receipt. We ended up by taking the paper table cloth on which the waitress had recorded our fare in pen and presenting it with our expenses claim on our return – well, it was proof of purchase, albeit unconventional.

In keeping with the island theme, I also travelled to Dublin in Ireland with a colleague while a detective sergeant at Truro to collect a prisoner who had been arrested at Shannon and brought to Dublin on a charge of criminal damage, an offence that had been committed in the Truro area. This occasion is memorable for the fact that the Irish Police – or Garda Síochána, as they are known – put me, my colleague and the prisoner onto a plane that we subsequently realised was bound for the United States and not Bristol. A catastrophe was gladly averted and the correct plane was soon identified. Mind you, we had received fantastic hospitality from our Irish counterparts the night before at the Dublin Police Club and had consumed vast quantities of Guinness. All's well that ends well!

Throughout my career I maintained my membership of the St John Ambulance (Cornwall and later Devon) and also, as a member of the Cornwall and later Devon and Cornwall Constabulary's first-aid team, I regularly competed in, judged and organised many local, regional and national police and other first-aid competitions. I also served on a national police working party reviewing 'First Aid in the Police Service', visiting many police forces in the UK, including the Royal Ulster Constabulary (RUC) in Belfast. The group's final recommendations were fully endorsed by the Association of Chief Police Officers.

I also revisited Belfast on one other occasion when I was temporarily attached to the personnel department at Exeter, where I had been charged with reviewing 'Sickness in the Police Service'. Like the Garda Síochána, the RUC was most hospitable and living and working among them showed only too clearly to me what a difficult job they had to do. I made many friends in the RUC and still keep in touch with some – particularly James Baxter, who was the police commander in Omagh at the time of the bombings in 1998. He was awarded the Queen's Police Medal for his service to policing and is now retired. He was and still is a true gentleman and recently served a term as the High Sheriff of County Tyrone.

As an aside, I also flew to Manchester with the Devon and Cornwall Constabulary's medical officer during my research into

'Sickness in the Police Service' and had the misfortune to be a passenger on our return flight to Exeter when we had to return to Manchester Airport because of an engine failure. All's well that ends well, but when I rang my wife to say I was having to stay overnight she didn't appear to be that pleased – she was of the view that I had planned an overnight stop. It wasn't until her sister, Lyn, who lives in Formby, rang her that night having heard on the local TV news that a plane, en route to Exeter, had been forced to return to Manchester with engine failure that she knew she had made a serious mistake. I arrived home safely next day to a sort of apology!

On my first visit to Belfast I was billeted in a police section house in the centre of the city and beside my bed was a poster setting out what action to take in the event of a mortar-bomb attack. The section house was also guarded by police officers carrying machine guns, as was the Police Federation Club that we visited for a meal. This was a surreal and unique experience for me, it has to be said, but starkly brought home the reality of policing in Northern Ireland at that time.

Lundy Island, off the coast of North Devon, was also visited by me during my time as an inspector at Ilfracombe. Tragically, a young woman had fallen down a cliff on the island and subsequently died of her injuries. My immediate boss, Chief Inspector Stan Dibble, and I flew out to initiate inquiries on behalf of the coroner and take statements. It was a bit unusual for senior officers to deal with such an incident, but rank does have its privileges when it comes to playing with the big boys' toys! The Devon and Cornwall Constabulary had not long had access to a police helicopter and the powers that be insisted that we use this as a means of getting to Lundy despite a hitherto and excellent local arrangement with the 22 Rescue Squadron at RAF Chivenor. Although Stan and I actually made it, after three days waiting to fly and being denied because of iffy weather on two days, it did cause quite a bit of mirth among the 22 Rescue Squadron crew who had been flying at will each and every day! It was something to do with an obscure aeronautical regulation associated with flying over water.

CHAPTER 21

THE EPILOGUE

The Isles of Scilly has not always been allied to Cornwall in policing terms. Prior to 1947 it had its own police force, and during my period based there I met the last surviving Isles of Scilly police officer, who was very much alive and kicking. His name was Eric Guy and he skippered the pleasure boat *Southern Queen*. I regret now not having pursued a closer relationship with him as I am sure he would have had a good tale or two to tell. Unfortunately he passed away in the 1970s.

I have, however, recently made contact with his daughter, Val Balkwill, who runs a small general store in Old Town. Val has presented his police-issue truncheon to the Isles of Scilly Museum, but still possesses one of his former police logbooks, which records misdemeanours committed by locals who still have relatives alive and living on St Mary's today – for this reason she is loath to put it in the public domain, for now at least.

Val also possesses a paper cutting (that was clearly published sometime between 1941 and 1947) where it was said that her father, Sergeant 7 Eric Guy, together with Constable W. Hurrell, were considered an efficient police force for the 1,749 people who grew daffodils on the 140 Isles of Scilly, twenty-five miles south-west of Land's End until 1941, when Sergeant Guy resigned to join the Merchant Navy, and Cornwall sent a sergeant and two constables on loan. It is not known what happened to Constable (Bill) Hurrell.

It is clear from the paper cutting that it was published at a time when the 'borrowed' sergeant and constables had returned to

144

the mainland (it is presumed after the end of the Second World War) and that the islands' joint police committee had asked for Cornwall to continue to police the islands. The article added that ex-Sergeant Guy was expected home soon and that the Isles of Scilly Council would petition the Home Secretary to preserve its independent force. The petition, it would seem, praised the ex-sergeant and referred therein to 'our earnest wish to reinstate him'. The newspaper article is headed 'Give us back our sergeant'. It is not clear, with any certainty, if this state of affairs was ever achieved; Val Balkwill thinks not.

It is a fact, however, that the Cornwall Constabulary took over policing of the islands in 1947 and that I would eventually join a list of exclusive, privileged and honoured police officers to be posted to such a beautiful, unique, inimitable and special part of the country – Scillybeat!

Sergeant Eric Guy, Isles of Scilly Police circa 1941.

I have also come across the names of two other former Scillonian police officers, Jack Hancock and Bill Earl, although it is likely, in my view and that of some locals, that Bill Earl and Bill Hurrell are one and the same person, their surnames sounding very similar when articulated in the local dialect. I have also been told of police lodgings at a house called, I believe, Raduna which is opposite the Scillonian Club near the park on the Parade.

Every posting I had in my career had its rich rewards and many periods of despair, despondency and the inevitable quick learning curve, but none was more satisfying, rewarding and life changing than my six months on the Isles of Scilly in 1966. I had arrived as a young police officer who lacked confidence and self-esteem and was most wary of working alone; but I left as a mature officer who was more than equipped for the big wide world and had the confidence and assurance to take up all the wonderful opportunities that became available to me within the force from a specialisation and promotion viewpoint.

There is no doubt that the 'Fortunate Islands' have left an indelible mark on my heart and I am constantly torn between spending the rest of my life there or not. Maybe one day, but it will very much depend on the lottery that Gill is convinced we are going to win! It is said that we all need dreams – this is obviously Gill's and mine – Gill quite recently even selected the house she wanted to buy and live in and decided how she would give it a makeover!

Gill and I are constantly counting the days to our next visit and I frequently, I am sure, bore her, my sons and friends with many anecdotal stories of my experiences while working and visiting the Scillies – they say that the older I get the better the stories become – it's a bit like the saying the older I get the better I was!

Regrettably, policing on the Isles of Scilly seems as far removed now as it could be from how it was when I served there – much has changed for the good, but some changes I see as retrograde steps. There is, for example, a much more modern and fit-for-purpose police station. It consists of two incorporated houses that serve as the homes for the resident sergeant and constable and their families, an office, two cells (with underfloor heating), an interview room and quarters on the ground floor for up to three single police officers. Having said 'more modern', it was purpose-built and first occupied in 1974, but at that time it was a far cry from the old days (my days, for example), with all mod cons and fabulous views over Hugh Town, and Porthcressa and Town Beaches. This new building cost £42,000 and was opened on 11th September 1974 in the presence of a large number of dignitaries, including Alderman Sam Ellis, chairman of the island's council, Mr N. Galbraith, HM Inspector of Constabularies, and John Alderson, Chief Constable of the Devon and Cornwall Police.

Just as a matter of interest, the first house for the police on the Isles of Scilly was provided in 1898 when the construction of fortifications required extra policemen; it appears to have had a bedroom and kitchen utensils and little else. At that time the local police were paid about £15 per annum, although it soon rose to the princely sum of £40 on the basis that they should also take over the responsibilities of lamplighter, caretaker of public buildings, town clock winder, school attendance officer and sanitary inspector – what a job description! By 1904, the pay for the two basic police officers on St Mary's was £52 per annum.

About the time of the First World War, cells were situated in the vicinity of the present Isles of Scilly Steamship Company office in Hugh Town, there being no official police station. The same building, I am advised, also housed local council officials and staff and acted as a courthouse.

The current police officers are now provided with a 4 × 4 police vehicle; regrettably you hardly ever see an officer on foot patrol these days (much like the mainland, I suppose), even though they have a Police Community Support Officer in addition to their complement of regular officers and no doubt some specials. I appreciate that this might be seen by some as sour grapes or an unnecessary criticism on the basis that I am no longer in the know, but the locals who speak to me on a regular basis and express similar viewpoints can't all be wrong.

I am afraid that I am now old school and somewhat curmudgeonly – I am allowed to be at my age – but I guess you become what you 'grow, inspire and value'. Policing in the 1960s era was fun, enjoyable and very rewarding, and anybody who is a fan of the ITV police series *Heartbeat* and *Heartbeat*'s spin-off, *The Royal*, will know what I mean.

I am sure, however, that whatever the current breed of police officers does on the Isles of Scilly they are doing it because they feel it is the appropriate way to go about their business – as we did, to be fair. Community policing, however, is all about getting out and about and mixing with the community and most of all being seen.

Many, I am sure, will have keenly watched the BBC TV series entitled *Island Parish* that was centred around the Isles of Scilly a year or so ago. I certainly did, and saw many of the characters I have mentioned in this book. I distinctly remember watching one particular episode when a young police officer stationed there spoke about policing and 'days gone by' and said something like "They even had a police launch here in the olden days." My immediate reaction was to retort, "Well, in that case I must have been there in prehistoric times as a police launch followed my posting!" I believe that just after I had left the islands the police did get access to a small punt and outboard engine, but rarely used it. It could have been quite dangerous to have gone out in a small boat without the necessary training and nautical know-how, although I have seen police ribs in the harbour at St Mary's at times when security was paramount – say, a royal visit, or when the force's Underwater Search Unit was in place on a training exercise.

I must sign off now and get off my soapbox as I wouldn't wish this *Scillybeat* biography of mine to be soured or misinterpreted. It is purely a memoir of mine of a time in my life that was so special and memorable and that is still having a marked and manifest impression on me after fifty years.

In my dotage, and especially during my retirement, I have been fortunate to travel the world and visit countries such as New Zealand, Australia, Fiji, Tahiti/Moorea, the Cook Islands, China, Hong Kong, Peru, Bolivia, Argentina, Brazil, Singapore, Kenya, South Africa, USA, Canada, most of the islands of the Caribbean and many European countries and none of them has come up to the way I feel about the Isles of Scilly – maybe New Zealand! The Isles of Scilly are unique, unsurpassed and peerless in every sense and are totally the opposite of what their title implies – there is nothing silly about the Isles of Scilly. In fact, many locals dislike the term 'Scillies' for this very reason, and although I have probably erred somewhere in this book I have not done so intentionally. In fact, following some recent research it would appear that the term 'Isles of Scilly' became the fashion in the early 1900s when C. J. King, the chemist and photographer at the time, pushed for the islands to be called the Isles of Scilly because a lot of post was being mistakenly sent to Sicily. King thought that by changing to the Isles of Scilly (from the Scillies) would ensure the postal service improved. (Source: Article by Alfie Trenear of St Mary's in *The Islander Magazine* autumn/winter 2011.)

To quote a recent Isles of Scilly Tourist Information Booklet:

> The Isles of Scilly lie just off the coast of Cornwall but seem like a world apart. Everyone who visits here falls in love. You might not put your finger on it right away, or it may be a mixture of emotions. But either way, we know that when you arrive, you will have the time of your life, and when it's time to go, you'll be yearning for more.

It is without doubt a truly inimitable place, geographically pleasing and beautiful in all weathers – it is said to have its own microclimate – and here the pace of life is much suited to a sedentary and relaxing lifestyle.

It is a place where no timepiece is necessary; the time of the day can be judged by the arrival and departure of the pleasure boats and *Scillonian*, the rising and setting of the sun, the tidal ebb and flow, the arrival of Skybus and the opening and closing of the shops. Many still close on Sundays, even in the summer holiday period!

I will conclude with a couple of sayings, neither of which are entirely unique or original, but summarise my feelings: "You can take the man from the Scillies but not the Scillies from the man" and "The Scillies might be known as the Fortunate Islands – well, I was fortunate to have worked, lived and played there and long may this continue."

Romeo, **O**scar, **G**olf, **E**cho, **R**omeo
and
Oscar, **U**niform, **T**ango.

APPENDIX A

HISTORY OF POLICING OF THE ISLES OF SCILLY (1890–1947)

This article is produced with grateful thanks to Wyn Grant, part-time professor of politics at the University of Warwick who has investigated Scilly's past at the National Archives at Kew and has gladly agreed for this 'History of Policing of the Isles of Scilly' to be reproduced in this book. Wyn is a regular visitor to the Isles of Scilly and contributes to articles published in the Scilly Now and Then *magazine and Radio Scilly.*

The Islands Get a Police Force

The Isles of Scilly Police Order of 1890 provided for the establishment of a police authority on the islands. In 1891 the parish constable appointed by the Select Vestry of St Mary's was transferred to the Isles of Scilly police force.

In the 1890's the islands were designated as a 'defended port' and a number of works were undertaken. In 1898, the employment of additional police in the Isles of Scilly was thought to be necessary 'consequent upon the men engaged in the construction of the new forts in these islands.'

As always, Mr Dorrien-Smith was an energetic lobbyist on behalf of the islands and made it clear that he wanted the matter settled in the following week when he would be in London. It was said that the contractor would be liable to pay the local authorities for the expense of any additional police which it might be necessary to employ to maintain order among the workman. In this case the War Office was effectively the contractor. The War Office felt 'obliged' to accept the cost of the extra police necessary so employed as a charge against 'Army Votes.'

Mr Dorrien-Smith wanted three Metropolitan Police officers brought in, but this was not possible. It was then suggested that it might be an attractive posting for retired officers, but no one came forward. In those days the islands were seen as a remote and isolated community.

The file records, 'The Secretary of State can only suggest that if it is not thought advisable to apply to the Cornish or other police forces, some of the engineers or foreman of the workmen engaged in constructing the forts might be sworn in as special constables. Such men would probably have more influence over the labourers than ordinary constables.' The eventual solution was to bring in three officers from the Royal Ulster Constabulary.

Before long, 'The number of navvies employed has now been reduced to forty-four and are not likely to increase.' It was suggested, 'that the number to be paid for by the War Office be reduced from three to one.' The last constable left in May 1901 and was sent to Dublin.

New Challenges for the Islands' Police

The First World War brought new challenges for the police force in the islands. Mr Dorrien-Smith reported in August 1915: 'We have one sergeant, and an assistant, when required, which is ample for our local requirements. We now have some five to 600 men from armed trawlers and drifters which come in and out of the place and are stationed here, also about sixty regulars under an officer to look after the wireless telegraph station and to guard over the naval stores.'

He continued 'Up to the present everything has been orderly, there was however some little trouble in getting the men out of the public houses. Some of the trawler men are very tough and unaccustomed to discipline. The drifter men are much more orderly. The public houses are only open from twelve to one and five to nine.' It was decided that one non-commissioned officer and four privates of the Royal Marines would be sent as a military police force.

In 1920, Arthur Dorrien-Smith, styling himself as the Governor of the islands stated that the local police force consisted of one man only. The islands needed protection against 'the riotous crew of a vessel'. The islands were also 'open to marauders.'

Civil servants thought that Mr Dorrien-Smith was confusing the defence of the islands and the maintenance of internal law and order. The War Office considered that all that was needed was a small force of special constables armed with revolvers. If the islanders wanted an additional police officer, then they should appoint one.

The file was then not opened again for fifteen years when the Home Office suddenly realised that there was a police force on the islands about which they knew very little. A civil servant wrote, 'I have been unable to find any trace of an inspection of this police force or any control over it having been exercised by the Secretary of State . . . In fact, our knowledge of this force appears to be very sketchy. When it was last heard of in 1921, it consisted of one constable. As the clerk's letter speaks of the sergeant and constables, the force must now consist of at least three men. Such a private police force, more independent of the Central Government even than the City of London police force, is a complete anomaly.'

'The most obvious remedy for the current anomaly is that Cornwall should police the Isles, but I imagine that local sentiment in the Isles would be dead against this abdication.'

Should the Islands Have a Chief Constable?

By 1938 the police force on the Isles of Scilly consisted of one sergeant and one constable. In 1938 the Home Office were asked about the appointment of a Chief Constable. It became apparent that Major Dorrien-Smith wanted to be appointed to this office.

The Home Office noted, 'It seems that the Scilly police are not a force with which we at the Home Office are much concerned and that they are in a singular position.' However, prompted by the request, they had to seek legal advice on what the position might be. They also started to investigate what was happening on the islands.

What they found concerned them, 'It appears that Major Dorrien-Smith, as chairman of the Joint Police Committee, advises the police force on the institution of criminal proceedings in certain cases and, subsequently, as chairman of the magistrates, adjudicates with other magistrates upon the cases. This practice is rightly felt to be wrong, since the same person should not be prosecutor and judge.' From a subsequent document, it became apparent that this state of affairs was greatly resented by the islanders.

The request to appoint a chief constable was given short shrift, but Major Dorrien-Smith returned to the attack, insisting 'At present it is understood that I do act as Chief Constable for the Islands vis a vis the CID London.' It was far from clear whether the services of Scotland Yard had ever been called for on the islands.

The Home Office was by this time getting more than a little exasperated by the time being taken up by this correspondence and concluded, 'In fact it seems very doubtful whether the matter is a very serious one as recent crime statistics reveal very few crimes for the islands, namely:

1933 one assault, six minor non indictable offences

1934 one case of larceny

1935 one assault, two minor non indictable offences

1936 Nil'

The usual stance of government departments towards the islands at this time was one of benign neglect. It was simply too much trouble to sort out the anomalous situations on the islands.

Indeed, in earlier Home Office files they are treated in the same category as the Channel Islands. It was the Second World War and its aftermath which led to big changes in policing and other aspects of island life. The islands could no longer be left to their own devices.

Cornwall Takes Over Policing the Islands

In 1940 the Police Committee for the islands represented that, as a result of billeting and other work arising from the presence of military forces, and of the increase of unoccupied property in the Islands, the existing force of one man was inadequate. The cost of an additional constable at £3 a week would be equivalent to a 7.5d rate. They therefore asked for financial help and their arguments received a sympathetic reception from the Home Office which recommended a grant of £100 a year.

The Treasury was unmoved, 'It seems to me that they ought to take their choice between paying the County rate (10.62d) or remaining an independent entity and meeting the cost of the additional man out of their own pockets – we do not see quite why the Scilly Isles should be given preferential treatment.'

As a compromise a sergeant was seconded from the Penzance force. In 1941 the Chief Constable of Penzance commandeered a motor torpedo boat and went to the islands where he received a cool reception. His report contained gratuitous remarks about various prominent individuals such as 'is no use during a raid' or 'is obviously fond of company and on occasion drinks too much'.

However, he reserved his most severe criticisms for the police, 'This service is one of the worst on the islands. The Sergeant has resigned and has not been replaced. The constable (an untrained man of nearly sixty years of age and with short police experience) now deals with police matters. His position is exceedingly difficult unless he takes the line of least resistance.'

It was agreed in 1941 (implemented in 1942) that the policing of the Isles would be carried out by the Cornwall Constabulary for the duration of the war. After war the Council decided that they would like the islands to be policed by the Cornwall County force. It had been found that 'since the present agreement with Cornwall, the policing of the Islands had been more efficient and cost less.'

There was some opposition from Alderman Nance to amalgamation on the grounds that 'Scillonians had a natural prejudice against outside interference.' Major Dorrien-Smith noted that 'Mr Nance is attempting to sabotage the scheme as I knew he would.' However, a merger had clear advantages and the order bringing it about was approved in March 1947.

Footnote: Professor Wyn Grant, who carried out this research at Kew, summarises by saying, 'Civil servants in London always found the situation of the islands baffling and anomalous, but they did not want to spend too much time and effort sorting it out so often matters were left to drift. This was particularly the case in relation to policing when levels of crime on the islands were very low. The Second World War provided the impetus to bring policing under the control of Cornwall.'

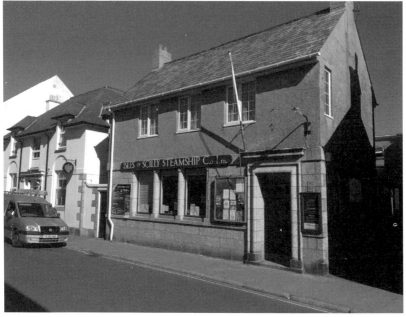

The Isles of Scilly Steamship Company office in Hugh Town, St Mary's; site of former police cells, courtroom and council offices – see Chapter 21.

APPENDIX B

HISTORY OF THE CORNWALL CONSTABULARY (1857–1967)

This article is produced with grateful thanks to Ken Searle, the author of a book entitled *One & All: A History of Policing in Cornwall*. Ken Searle, a Cornishman born and bred, joined the Cornwall Constabulary in 1958 and served at Penzance, Egloskerry, Saltash and Pool. Ken spent years researching and collecting photographs charting the history of the police force in Cornwall from its founding in 1857 through to its amalgamation with the Devonshire (and Plymouth/Exeter City) Police Force in 1967.

The Cornwall County Constabulary was formed in February 1857 following the passing of the County and Borough Police Act 1856. Its original complement of police officers was 179.

The County and Borough Police Act 1856 directed the justices in every county to establish an efficient police force.

The Cornwall County Constabulary absorbed Bodmin Borough Police (one officer) in 1865, Liskeard Borough Police (one officer) in 1877, Launceston Borough Police (one officer) in 1883, Falmouth Borough Police (four officers), Helston Borough Police (one officer), Penryn Borough Police (two officers) and St Ives Borough Police (one officer) in 1889, Truro City Police (thirteen officers) in 1921, and Penzance Borough Police (twenty-four officers) and the Isles of Scilly Police in 1947.

From 1947 it was officially called the Cornwall and Isles of Scilly Constabulary, although this name was rarely used.

On 1st June 1967 it amalgamated with Devon and Exeter Police and Plymouth City Police to form the Devon and Cornwall Constabulary. The Cornwall Constabulary on amalgamation had 476 police officers. Most Cornish Officers named the new force the Cornwall and Devon Constabulary.

In many of the police forces formed throughout the 1800s the various committees looked at the military for leaders and this was the case in Cornwall when Colonel Walter Raleigh Gilbert, CB, was appointed as Chief Constable (1857–1896). It is not surprising, therefore, that a military-orientated approach ensued with a sergeant major, strict discipline, and police stations with rooms defined as guardrooms.

The next Chief Constable, R. Middleton Hill Esq. (1896–1909) brought about a major stage in the administration of the force; he was instrumental in producing a book of instructions for the force, entitled *Rules and Regulations for the Guidance of the Cornwall Constabulary*, that was issued to each member of the force in 1900. It became known as *The Black Book*.

Under the heading 'Beat Duty' it outlined, for example:

> Every Constable, when his usual hours of patrol are over, will return to his home and remain there taking necessary rest and unless called out to perform some serious service (the nature of which must be reported by him) it is expected that he will be found at his lodgings until the hour of going on duty again. No Constable is permitted to be absent from his beat except on duty or by permission of the Superintendent.

Under the heading 'Conditions of Service' appears the following:

> Any Constable who shall marry without first obtaining the permission of the Chief Constable will be liable to dismissal.

It will be noted by reading the above *Black Book* extracts that many of the rules and regulations appear to be draconian in their severity, but they appear to have worked and many were maintained for years in some form or other.

There were only six men who held the office of Chief Constable of the Cornwall Constabulary (1857–1967), eight Deputy Chief Constables who held the rank of superintendent (1857–1942) and four Assistant Chief Constables (1943–1967).

The author of *Scillybeat*'s great-grandfather, Superintendent William H. Beare, was Deputy Chief Constable for the period 1902–1910. He was appointed to the force on 3rd October 1864 and was promoted to first-class constable (1872), sergeant (1883), inspector (1891) and finally superintendent/Deputy Chief Constable (1902). He was stationed at Bodmin, Helston, Penzance, Truro, Bodmin, Helston, Falmouth and again Bodmin, retiring on 3rd September 1910.

In the King's Birthday Honours List of 1909, Deputy Chief Constable W. H. Beare was awarded the King's Police Medal. The Chief Constable, at that time, said, "I am glad to take the opportunity on behalf of the force in congratulating Deputy Chief Constable Beare on the well-deserved award bestowed on him which is an honour not only to the Deputy Chief Constable but also to the whole force."

Throughout its history the Cornwall Constabulary was generally held in high esteem by the public and adjoining forces despite the historical, inbred and somewhat flippant rivalry between the Cornish and Devonians.

To be honest, this frivolous relationship between the Cornish and English is not meant too literally – it is suspected that there is more respect and admiration for each other than each is prepared to outwardly admit.

There is, however, a Cornish proverb that says, 'The further you go east the more certain you are that the Wise Men never came from there!' Maybe this sums up this irreverent liking versus loathing between the Cornish and their neighbours, the Devonians, or is it a final dig from a man of Cornish origin but with an English birthright!

To conclude this appendix I would like to set out the oath that was sworn by officers joining the police force, and which I swore before a magistrate on joining the Cornwall Constabulary in 1966:

I, (Roger William Jacob) do swear that I will well and truly serve our Sovereign Lady the Queen, in the office of Constable for the County of Cornwall, without favour or affection, malice or ill will; and that I will, to the best of my power, cause the peace to be kept and preserved and prevent all offences against the persons and properties of Her Majesty's subjects; and that while I continue to hold the said office, I will, to the best of my skill and knowledge, discharge all the duties thereof faithfully, according to the law, so help me God.

Superintendent William H. Beare (circa 1900).

APPENDIX C

THE AUTHOR'S BACKGROUND

Roger (William) Jacob was born on 21st September 1944 at the North Devon Infirmary, Barnstaple. The NDI has long since been demolished and a block of flats now sits in its place. Oddly enough, Roger and his wife, Gill, now live almost within sight of the former NDI and have done so since 1988.

Roger's parents, William (Bill) Henry Jacob from Newquay and Muriel Beatrice Jacob (née Whitting) of Fowey, lived at the time in a bedsit in Bicton Street, Barnstaple. Bill was in the RAF and was stationed at RAF Chivenor, near Braunton. This is how Roger became the subject of dual nationality, Cornish by parentage and English by birth!

Roger was brought up in Newquay, Cornwall, living with his parents and sister, Pauline, at 43 Crantock Street, Newquay. He attended Newquay Boys' Grammar School, later to merge with the Newquay Girls' Grammar School, leaving at the age of eighteen years having attained six O levels and two A levels. Later in life he attained a further A level, in law, having attended a night school in Barnstaple.

He initially, because of his St John Ambulance background, had the intention of becoming a radiographer – and did a short placement at Truro City Hospital – but eventually decided to join the Cornwall Constabulary. Perhaps his short encounter with radiography gave him the ability to see through people that stood him in good stead during his policing career!

Roger joined the local Newquay St John Ambulance Brigade

as a cadet, as did his sister, Pauline. Their father, Bill, was the superintendent of the Newquay Division and their mother, Muriel, a supporter. Roger was part of a very successful St John Ambulance cadet first-aid team, competing in county, regional and national first-aid competitions – he also performed duties during the summer season at a St John Ambulance beach hut that was situated on Towan Beach, Newquay.

At the age of seventeen years, having joined the St John Ambulance adult division, he regularly performed full-time ambulance 'on-call' duties on a Tuesday night (7 p.m. to 7 a.m.) together with a senior member who drove the ambulance – Roger acted as the attendant. In those days the full-time ambulance service only worked from Monday to Friday from 7 a.m. to 7 p.m., and the St John Ambulance covered the remaining days and hours, all voluntary. When the service became full-time, many of the St John Ambulance members joined as paid ambulance officers.

Roger was also a member of the St Michael's Parish Church Choir, Newquay, as was his sister and father. He sang on one occasion at a Royal School of Church Music Festival Service at St Paul's Cathedral, London, with a colleague and two members of the Truro Cathedral Choir. He also competed in the Cornwall Music Festival at Indian Queens as a boy soprano and won a bronze medallion for his rendition. All this choral singing stood him in good stead for the years ahead, although his voice did break, thankfully, and he has since adopted a tenor voice!

Roger spent thirty-two years as a police officer and retired as a substantive chief inspector/acting superintendent in 1995. Although he had passed his promotion board for selection for superintendent, the Sheehy Inquiry – an inquiry set up by the government to review police ranks – intervened and an alternative career opportunity, coupled with being able to draw down his pension, helped him to focus his mind and make the decision to retire and move on.

He spent his entire police career working throughout Devon and Cornwall. Although at one time he seriously considered applying for a CID role in the Cayman Islands, had a more than passing interest in joining the Royal Hong Kong Police and was approached towards the end of his career to consider taking up a police training role in Pakistan, he never looked to move outside the West Country or be too far from God's Country – Cornwall of course.

Roger attended a number of specialist training courses during his time as an inspector/chief inspector at the Police Staff College, Bramshill, Hampshire – the staff college was known irreverently within the service as 'Brands Hatch'. He was also selected for interview for a course in criminology at Cambridge University and invited to attend a selection process to be a member of the directing staff at Bramshill specialising in career development – both were unsuccessful. Every cloud has a silver lining as Roger most certainly preferred operational duties that meant living at home and not out of a suitcase.

During his police career he was fortunate to meet a number of members of the royal family. As a young sergeant at Truro he became a member of the inaugural Prince's Trust (Cornwall) Committee, meeting Prince Charles at a reception in Newquay – he later went on to meet Prince Charles on two other occasions, once when Prince Charles was visiting St Mawes and again on a royal visit to Devon when he was a detective inspector and in charge of local security. He also met Princess Anne when she officially opened the new police station at Truro and was part of the Queen's local security team when she visited Truro Cathedral as part of her silver-jubilee celebrations in 1977.

Roger also met the Queen and Duke of Edinburgh when they visited the St John Ambulance National Headquarters at Clerkenwell, London, as part of St John's nonacentenary celebrations in 1999. He has also attended two garden parties at Buckingham Palace with his wife Gill in connection with his police and St John Ambulance roles. Finally, Roger was instrumental in getting Princess Margaret to attend and officially open the new Barnstaple St John Headquarters, known as Braddon House, in 2000. It is believed that this was one of Princess Margaret's last pubic engagements before she died in 2002.

Since retiring from the police, Roger has worked as the chief executive of St John Ambulance, Devon (1995–2000), served as joint vice chairs of the North Devon Community Health Council (2000–2003) and the North Devon Public and Patient Involvement Forum (2003–2004), and as clerk to Instow Parish Council in North Devon (2000–2013). In this last-mentioned position he attained Quality Parish Council Clerk status.

He is currently a member of the (St John) Priory Chapter based at Clerkenwell, London, the chair of Devon's County Priory Group and county president of St John (Devon). In his role as county president he has met, on many occasions, Sophie, Princess of Wessex, GCVO, who is the Grand President of St John.

Roger's fascination with island life has also extended to his voluntary St John career in that in 2008 he visited Barbados in the Caribbean and forged a partnership between Devon and Barbados St John. This partnership continues to thrive to the present day and Roger has visited the island twice since, once on a holiday cruise and on another occasion to run a 'governance' workshop with Barbados St John Council members and supporters. He also used this opportunity to launch a Barbados St John Band, having previously provided them with musical instruments from the UK and an ambulance to further their life-saving mission.

For his work within St John, totalling fifty-eight years, he is the holder of a Long Service Medal and Laurel Leaf bar that depicts fifty-two years eligible service. He is also a member of the Order of St John at the rank of commander, a position he was appointed to in 1996. He was most honoured to receive this accolade from the Lord Lieutenant of Cornwall, Lady Mary Holborow – a former Cornwall County St John Commissioner – at a ceremony held on St Michael's Mount, Cornwall.

Roger is also a member of the church choir at St Peter's and Mary Magdalene's Parish Church, Barnstaple (1995–present day), Artavian Singers (2009–present day) and Amalfi Singers (1995–present day), a trustee of the Barnstaple and North Devon Dispensary Trust (2010–present day) and a member of the Fremington Quay Heritage Centre's Environment Group (2010–present day). He also finds time to play golf at Saunton, toil in his garden and walk his dog, Bryher, with his wife, Gill, enjoying the many beautiful countryside walks around North Devon.

Roger's ambition and long-term goal has always been to commit to paper his love and fondness for the Isles of Scilly and to record, for posterity's sake, the many stories that he has countlessly, and probably boringly on occasions, recounted to his family and friends. Hopefully, however, when he is a long and distant memory in the minds of his family – especially his grandchildren, Will, Xander and Imogen – they will be able to open this memoir and have a chuckle or two and at the same time toast his health and remember him with fondness and affection. Roger would most certainly have liked to have known more about his great-grandfather's career in the Cornwall Constabulary. There is no doubt that he would have had many a good story to tell well beyond what is already recorded in this book.

Roger dedicates this book to his parents, Bill and Muriel, who sadly missed his adult life and from which they would hopefully have derived a great sense of pride, gratification and happiness. He would also like to dedicate this memoir to his many friends on the Isles of Scilly, past and present, particularly his early 'life mentor', Guthrie Pender, and now his son Joe who ribs him something rotten about his current 'old' age and infirmity – and that's coming from a man who is quickly approaching his fiftieth birthday.

Finally, this book is a record of Roger's fond memories of working and visiting the Isles of Scilly, interspersed with his other career and life experiences, and a heartfelt tribute to the Scillonian community that is, for him, so special and unique in every sense of the word.

Long may the Isles of Scilly remain so!

ACKNOWLEDGEMENTS

In writing this memoir Roger would like to acknowledge the support and assistance provided by Professor Wyn Grant (contributor to *Scilly Now and Then*), Ken Searle (author of *One & All: A History of Policing in Cornwall*), Amanda Martin – curator of the Isles of Scilly Museum and chair of the Council of the Isles of Scilly, Amanda's colleagues at the Isles of Scilly Museum, the Islands' Partnership (for use of their map), Gibson's of Scilly (for permitting the reproduction of many of the pictures in the book), John Purchas (author of *Death on the Isles of Scilly*), Clive Mumford (editor of the *Scillonian Magazine*), June Lethbridge (for the picture of the *Sanu*), Peggy and Norman Discombe, Bill Pender, Joe Pender (for his photographs especially), the St Mary's Boatmen's Association, John Bourdeaux, Graham Andrews (newspaper reporter, friend and lover of all things Isles of Scilly), and all those members of his family who encouraged him to complete this project and spent many hours proofreading and vetting the many drafts along the way, and finally Richard Stockwell, Rose Nicholas and all their colleagues at Arthur H. Stockwell Ltd, for their guidance, support and patience in bringing this 'once in a lifetime' project to a pleasing conclusion.

*Bill and Muriel Jacob, taken at Trenance Boating Lake, Newquay,
circa 1960 – parents of Roger and Pauline.*

*Roger on steps of Truro Cathedral with HM Queen Elizabeth II during
her Silver Jubilee Tour in 1977 – see Appendix C.*

Roger being introduced to Charles, Prince of Wales at the inaugural meeting of the Prince's Trust (Cornwall) Committee circa 1976–7 see Appendix C.

Roger (rear centre left) and his colleague Sue Ayre of Ilfracombe St John (rear right) with members of Barbados St John Youth Band with instruments and ambulance donated by Devon St John – see Appendix C.

Transfer of passengers by rib to the beach at Rushy Bay, Bryher, at low tide from Sapphire.